A Hole in One

A
HOLE IN ONE

and Other
LIFELESSONS
from
Golf

NAVPRESS ◖
BRINGING TRUTH TO LIFE
P.O. Box 35001, Colorado Springs, Colorado 80935

OUR GUARANTEE TO YOU

We believe so strongly in the message of our books that we are making this quality guarantee to you. If for any reason you are disappointed with the content of this book, return the title page to us with your name and address and we will refund to you the list price of the book. To help us serve you better, please briefly describe why you were disappointed. Mail your refund request to: NavPress, P.O. Box 35002, Colorado Springs, CO 80935.

The Navigators is an international Christian organization. Our mission is to reach, disciple, and equip people to know Christ and to make Him known through successive generations. We envision multitudes of diverse people in the United States and every other nation who have a passionate love for Christ, live a lifestyle of sharing Christ's love, and multiply spiritual laborers among those without Christ.

NavPress is the publishing ministry of The Navigators. NavPress publications help believers learn biblical truth and apply what they learn to their lives and ministries. Our mission is to stimulate spiritual formation among our readers.

ISBN 1-57683-136-1

Cover design by Dan Jamison
Cover illustration by V. Smithson / Wood River Media, Inc.

Some of the anecdotal illustrations in this book are true to life and are included with the permission of the persons involved. All other illustrations are composites of real situations, and any resemblance to people living or dead is coincidental.

Scripture quotations in this publication are taken from the HOLY BIBLE: NEW INTERNATIONAL VERSION ® (NIV®). Copyright © 1973, 1978, 1984 by International Bible Society. Used by permission of Zondervan Publishing House. All rights reserved.

Printed in the United States of America

1 2 3 4 5 6 7 8 9 10 11 12 13 / 05 04 03 02 01 00 99

FOR A FREE CATALOG OF
NAVPRESS BOOKS & BIBLE STUDIES,
CALL 1-800-366-7788 (USA)
OR 1-416-499-4615 (CANADA)

*This book is dedicated to John Pearson
and Bob Kobielush, along with:*

*Dave Auker
Gary Fawver
Neil Fichthorn
Keith Hunt
Bob Kraning
Bob McDowell
Fred Miller
Brian Ogne
Mark Olson
Max Rice*

*and the others who gave so much to Christian
Camping International/USA during my years on
the Board of Directors.*

—DAN BOLIN

Contents

Preface

Is your spiritual life in the rough? Do you have a slice you can't seem to correct in your relationship with God? Do your putts seem to wind up short of the cup when it comes to spiritual commitments? Then you're like me most of the time, and I had you in mind during each step of the writing process.

When we have a bad round, we don't quit golf (but we may think about it). Instead, we go back and try again. That's the way God wants us to be in our walk with Him. He doesn't expect a hole-in-one on every shot; He doesn't even expect us to shoot par. He just wants us to keep trying to lower our score as best we can.

Don't get me wrong. God wants us to become like Him, and He certainly desires perfection. But He knows our tendency toward inconsistency and rebellion. The hope of this book is not perfection; rather, it's to move us a step closer to God and to lower our spiritual handicaps a stroke or two.

This book would still be a pile of paper scraps scattered across my desk—or ideas in the dark recesses of my mind—if not for the help and support of some great people. Steve Webb, Sue Geiman, and Gary Wilde all helped shape the ideas and walked me through to completion. My wife, Cay, and daughter, Haley, were great as usual. Their love and support were fundamental to the ideas that have finally taken shape on these pages. Thanks also to all the Bible teachers and preachers who have invested in my life over the years.

DAN BOLIN
December 1998

INTRODUCTION

Golf and my life seem to run on parallel tracks. I'm not as good as I wish, but I know those who are worse. I bounce back and forth between success and failure and between satisfaction and frustration. Golf has just enough pain and pleasure to make it resemble life all too closely.

One thing is certain: We don't get any better at golf unless we practice and play the game. Once a year doesn't cut it if we want to improve. It takes regular, intentional, focused effort to improve as a golfer, and the same can be said of improving our game as a Christian. Both golf and our walk with God can be fun, exciting, and rewarding. But both require an investment of regular time and energy if we want to move to the next level.

I wrote this book for the guy whose life is filled with challenge and whose schedule is filled with responsibilities, for the guy who wants to be better at golf but who knows he should be better at developing his faith in God as well. Deuteronomy 6:6 says, "These commandments that I give you today are to be upon your hearts." Going through the day with something on my heart means I'm thinking and pondering the issue when I get up, as I drive to work, while I eat lunch, and when I stop for gas or go to bed. I can't get it off my mind, even if I try. Why shouldn't we have God's Word—and our relationship with Him—on our hearts all day long?

The result of focusing our life on Christ is that His life will overflow into the lives of those closest to us. The next verse begins, "Impress them on your children. . . ." If we want to make an impression on our children, we must have the real deal in our own lives.

The intent of this book is not to make you a super saint or to ensure that you will make a godly impression on your children. No, my simple hope is that the stories and biblical insights will be on your heart throughout the day. If I can help you keep your heart focused on God, I'll consider it a hole in one.

Note to the Reader:
You can use this book in a variety of ways. Of course, you might choose to read a chapter a day for a month. Great! But don't limit yourself to that kind of rigorous reading plan if your schedule would tend to make it a chore. In that case, try these options:

- Read a chapter a week for thirty-one weeks, perhaps on a Saturday night before Sunday worship.
- Read chapters with a group of friends and discuss your reactions and insights together—whenever you can meet.
- Read every time you go golfing, or whenever you think about golfing.
- Read when the Spirit moves you.

Reading this book ought to be like taking a breath of fresh air whenever you need it. So no matter how you plan your devotional times, let them become quality visits with the Lord.

Bad Weather — Good Weather

We arrived at the course before 6:00 a.m. on the day of the tournament and kept telling ourselves that the sky was clearing to the west.

"Go ahead. Get things set up," I said as the volunteers and staff dutifully began to place banners and signs at the proper holes. Registration tables were set up. Coffee, juice, fruit, and donuts were in place, and shiny new ski-boats and cars were delivered to the par threes, where a hole-in-one would win you a great prize and place your name in the local headlines.

But there was no clearing to the west — or to the east, north, or south. Foul weather crept toward us, with towering, black clouds belching out thunderclaps, even as we prayed hard for sunshine. No rain was falling when the golfers went to their tees for the shotgun start, but within an hour the bottom dropped out. And soon everyone was running for cover.

Growing in the Rain?

We waited as long as possible, served lunch early, and then told people to come back in two weeks for the make-up tournament. Weeks and months of hard work had gone into lining up sponsors, bargaining for prizes, and filling the

13

tournament with more than two hundred golfers. We'd been ready to get the event behind us and move on to our next project, but the weather dictated that we do it all over again two weeks hence.

Why Lord? I don't need this, especially right now!

At times hassles and problems seem to be our constant companions. We need a break; we want some sunshine in our lives, but the rain keeps falling.

Maybe God has something more important in store than our ease and comfort. Maybe He wants us to learn some things from the school of rainstorms that we will never comprehend in the sunshine. Consider Romans 5:3-4:

> *We also rejoice in our sufferings, because we know that suffering produces perseverance; perseverance, character; and character, hope.*

We are told to rejoice in sufferings. The command is not to rejoice *because* of the sufferings; rather, we are to rejoice *within* them, knowing that God is on the move in our lives. He wants to do something special, and our temporary discomfort is worth the eternal results He desires.

The first result of suffering is *perseverance*. No one likes suffering. We want relief from our pain, and we want it now. Our strength wanes as we toil under ongoing tense relationships, crushing financial concerns, or medical problems that offer little hope. But as we persevere, we know God is *developing our character*, the second blessed result of our life's rainy weather.

The process of moving from suffering to perseverance, and

on to character development, applies to every area of life. Are you persevering in your commitments to purity at home and honesty at work? Are your marriage vows and promises to your children being fulfilled? Perseverance is the key.

Hope So!
As we rely upon God's faithfulness in today's storms, we'll be developing the character we need for the next rainstorm heading toward us early tomorrow morning. In other words, the record of God's help in the past inspires *hope*, the third potential result of our stormy times.

Hope is the final step in developing the character strength to handle the stresses of life. We may be expecting 18 holes of sunny weather, but at some point the bottom will fall out for every one of us. At those times, we'll need to do more than just run for cover. But what, exactly, will you do?

Check Your Scorecard
READ 1 THESSALONIANS 1:6-7

- In spite of suffering, the Thessalonians imitated Christ. What aspect of your lifestyle should be more Christlike, even though it may cause some pain to change?
- These early believers' response to suffering was an *internal* joy that could come only from the Holy Spirit. What was the *external* result of their suffering?

IN THE BAG

GOLF BAGS CONTAIN AN INTERESTING ASSORTMENT OF CLUBS AND equipment. There are woods for power, irons for various distances and lofts, a putter for delicate accuracy, and wedges for problems along the way. Besides the clubs, a bag has pockets — lots of pockets. Hidden in these compartments are tees, sleeves of balls, umbrellas, old score cards, tools to repair divots, ball markers, and maybe even a candy bar or two.

One bag holds many different pieces of equipment. Each piece is unique but each piece is essential to a golfer's success. What good is a putter if there is no driver or iron to get the ball to the green? What is the use of any club without the balls? What good is the ball without the clubs? Everything in the bag has value. Some appear to be more essential, but in any given situation a little-used piece of equipment will be just the thing to save the day.

So Much in Common

I think of that bag of clubs when I read Ephesians chapter four. Here we see one bag and a few essential "clubs"—seven basic doctrinal truths that all believers hold in common.

There is one body and one Spirit—just as you were called to one hope when you were called—one Lord, one faith, one baptism; one God and Father of all, who is over all and through all and in all. (verses 4-6)

The apostle Paul loved using the image of all Christians being a part of one, giant body. It works well because we all need each other. *One Spirit* unites us as He indwells, seals, teaches, guides, convicts, and supports believers in the daily events of the Christian life. His unique gifts are given to build up the entire body. Special gifts come to individual believers, but the Spirit Himself is common to all believers.

No matter how different our life experiences are, we Christians all share a common *hope* of eternal life with God Himself. Americans, Russians, Africans, Asians, rich, poor, educated, illiterate, male, female—we all share the same hope of eternal life.

The reference to *one Lord* reminds us of the only Savior available to us. One Lord eliminates any alternative that might challenge Jesus Christ for supremacy in our lives. Ultimately, our relationship to Jesus is the bond that unites all of us.

We share a common *faith*. This can refer to our subjective response to what God has done for us, or it can mean the body of truth that surrounds the core of the gospel. Either understanding reinforces the unity that we share as followers of Christ.

Baptism demonstrates to a watching world our identification with Christ in His death, burial, and resurrection. We share this common experience that binds us together.

The final source of unity is one God and Father of us all. We share the Holy Spirit, the Lord Jesus, and God the Father. The entire Trinity unifies us as we collectively live the Christian life.

Play Your Role

Each of us has a special role to play as we serve the Lord together for the good of our brothers and sisters in Christ and as we share His love and Word with those around us. Verse 7 says,

> To each one of us grace has been given as Christ apportioned it.

The passage goes on to list several gifts God provides His children. The bag is full of different clubs, each one suited for a special moment, ready for a special situation.

We share so much with other believers, and yet we often end up focusing on issues that divide rather than celebrating the glorious realities we share. We're so uniquely gifted, yet we expend so much effort trying to conform to one another or demanding that others be like us.

Let's just enjoy being in the bag together!

Check Your Scorecard
READ 1 PETER 4:10-11

- What are the two basic types of gifts mentioned in these verses? Which type of gift has God entrusted to you?
- What is one way you could use your gift this week?

THREE

CADDIES

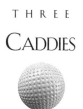

NEAR THE END OF MY SEVENTH-GRADE YEAR, MY BAND TEACHER, math teacher, and two homeroom teachers invited four of their star pupils to caddie for them on nine holes after school. The arrangements were made for us to ride to the course and carry the bags for the foursome. Our parents would pick us up later.

It was my first experience on a golf course, and I did little to help my band teacher; in fact, I probably cost him a few strokes — and several gray hairs!

He Comes Alongside

But good caddies are amazing people. They work hard, know the details of the course, provide encouragement and advice — all the while expecting none of the glory.

A caddie comes alongside a golfer to encourage, direct, and support the golfer. As Christians, we have a Helper who has come alongside each of us. In John 14 Jesus explained to His disciples that they should expect the Holy Spirit to come to their assistance. He said,

> *"I will ask the Father, and he will give you another Counselor to be with you forever — the Spirit of truth."* (verses 16-17)

The word *counselor* is sometimes translated "comforter," "helper," or "advocate." The Holy Spirit functions much like a caddie. He provides the help we need when we need it. Verse 26 captures more of the Holy Spirit's role.

"The Counselor, the Holy Spirit, whom the Father will send in my name, will teach you all things and will remind you of everything I have said to you."

These verses emphasize three wonderful things the Holy Spirit does—or is—on our behalf. First, the Spirit acts on behalf of the Father. We often thank the Father for sending His Son to earth to provide for our needs, but He also sent the Holy Spirit. The Father loves us so much that He sent His Son to provide salvation and He sent the Holy Spirit to help us meet the challenges of life. The Father knew we needed to establish a relationship with Him that only Jesus could arrange. But God also knew we had an equally huge need for assistance as we walk though the "the valley of the shadow of death" in this life.

Second, the Spirit is a long-term gift—He will be with us forever. We can quench the Spirit (1 Thessalonians 5:19), grieve Him (Ephesians 4:30), lie to Him (Acts 5:3), and be filled with alternatives to Him (Ephesians 5:18). But we can never free ourselves from God's wonderful gift. God knows that we need the Spirit most when we deserve Him the least. As Christians, we know that nothing can separate us from the Spirit's help and availability. There is no place and no time the Spirit is not on duty.

Third, a major job of the Spirit is to be our teacher. Through our own cognitive powers, we can learn some things about God, ourselves, and the world in which we live, but only God Himself can reveal to us the true meaning and purpose behind all that is. We normally think of teaching as transferring information in an academic sense. In reality, we need to learn much more than information. We must gain insights into our strengths and weaknesses, learn character, forgiveness, reconciliation, and sensitivity, as well as develop skills for ministry.

Our churches, Christian radio, camps and conferences, books, and Bible studies are all tools the Spirit uses to teach us. But He is not limited to these methods, for He can speak to our hearts and teach us directly. The Spirit works in our minds, bringing to remembrance a verse of Scripture, an encouraging word, a rebuke, or an insight that apart from Him would be lost in the dark recesses of our memory.

Life is tough. We often enter the tall grass with no clue as to where our ball is. But we have a Helper who comes alongside us. The Father has given us a Caddie who knows more about life's course than we do. He is aware of the dangers and can teach us the details of life to improve our game. And it is great to know that our Helper is with us forever.

Check Your Scorecard
READ 1 THESSALONIANS 5:19 AND EPHESIANS 4:30

- What sin or distraction is extinguishing the fire of the Holy Spirit in your life these days?
- What changes in thought, behavior, attitude, or pattern of life will keep you from grieving the Holy Spirit today?

CART PATHS

I KNOW IT WOULD BE BETTER IF I WALKED, BUT I'M A GOLF CART kind of guy. I seem to enjoy the quiet cart ride on a sunny spring day as much as I relish playing the game. Cart paths are great, but I have a compulsion to play commando with the cart and go "off road" whenever I have a chance.

The cart paths are there for a reason, of course. At times they provide the safest route for a golfer to get from one hole to the next, but usually their purpose is simply to protect the course, preserving its condition for the next golfer. Danger and destruction are the consequences of driving Rambo-style off the beaten path.

Holy Highway

Pathway imagery abounds in Scripture. The prophet Isaiah, for example, speaks of a highway as he predicts judgment and promises well-being to the Hebrew people. Chapter 35 describes future blessings for Israel, but the picture can apply to all of us today. Verses 8-9 state,

> *A highway will be there; it will be called the Way of Holiness. The unclean will not journey on it; it will be for those who walk in that Way; wicked fools will not go*

about on it. No lion will be there, nor will any ferocious
beast get up on it; they will not be found there. But only
the redeemed will walk there.

Highways provide direct access through natural terrain.
God's pathway allows us direct and unobstructed access to
Himself. Even though within the landscape of our lives we
encounter detours and obstacles that could keep us from relating
directly and easily with God, He has cut a pathway to us and
cleared the way so we can come to Him whenever we desire. He
provided the pathway to Himself through the death and resurrection of His Son. If we've entered into a relationship with Jesus,
then we're on the pathway that heads directly to the Father.

The name of this highway is The Way of Holiness. To
qualify for travel on this pathway, we must be holy. But that's
the problem, isn't it?

We know we don't qualify for access to this special road
because of our sinfulness. At the same time, we realize how
desperately we need to find an "on-ramp" because this highway
is the only hope we have. Without The Way of Holiness we're
lost and have no good options. The passage says, "The unclean
will not journey on it." Only as we appropriate the cleansing
God provides will we have access to this path. Only one on-
ramp is available, and it runs through the forgiveness Jesus has
won for us.

Wholly Healthy
What is the highway like? What should we expect on the
pathway God paves for us?

I know that wicked fools, lions, and other ferocious beasts won't be there. I'm always encountering people, pain, questions, temptations, and problems that resemble these forbidden foes. And my traveling companions seem to be worry, concern, fear, and frustration as much as peace, joy, and fulfillment. Somehow the fools and dangerous beasts have joined my journey. Yet the issue at hand is *the ultimate destination*. No distraction or danger will keep me from my ultimate goal. No foolish mistake or ferocious beast of a problem will stop me from reaching my ultimate destination of eternal fellowship with God.

Perspective itself helps us on this journey. Someone has said that ninety-five percent of the bad things we anticipate never come to pass. We tend to bring our own problems with us rather than trusting God to provide the security we need along the way.

Get on the cart path! On so many levels, it's the healthiest approach to living. The solid surface provides the best access over slippery ground. But danger and damage await everyone unwilling to use God's wonderfully safe pathway.

Check Your Scorecard
READ JOHN 14:1-6

- As a follower of Christ, what is your ultimate destination?
- What tempting off-ramps tend to hinder your spiritual journey? What helps you overcome these hindrances?

FIVE

CARTS AND WALKERS

WE YOUNG GUYS WERE IN A HURRY. AND WE DEFINITELY WANTED to get on the course before the two old guys with their pull carts. *We get stuck behind them, and we'll be here all day!*

They obliged us young bucks, and we stepped ahead to hit our tee shots down fairway number one. I was in the trees to the right, the others weren't much better, and we hacked our way through the brush, returning without our original balls (but with a few more than when we had started). We hit toward the green and again wandered around in the tall grass until we chipped ourselves closer and, eventually, onto the green.

We carded 6, 7, 8, 8. A pretty miserable start on the first par 4.

And how were the seniors doing? We were heading for the second tee when our friends with the pull carts sauntered up to the green and two-putted. By the time we'd sliced our next four drives into the woods, the old guys were waiting for us to clear out ahead of them.

They kept pushing us the rest of the way.

Playing It Straight
We offered them the opportunity to play through, but they seemed to be in no hurry. We were racing back and forth in our carts making

great time crossing the fairways and looking for lost balls, and they just kept coming straight down the fairway with their pull carts in machine-like precision. They weren't powerful. They just kept playing straight and being persistent.

The Bible tells of a man who played it straight and wouldn't give up, even while the rest of the world was rushing around in rebellion and pushing the limits of God's patience. Noah lived in a social climate similar to our own. Genesis 6:5-6 gives this account:

> *The LORD saw how great man's wickedness on the earth had become, and that every inclination of the thoughts of his heart was only evil all the time. The LORD was grieved that he had made man on the earth, and his heart was filled with pain.*

It appeared that evil had won the day. Everyone on earth had turned away from God. Every thought of every person was totally wicked. What a mess! If I'd been looking down from heaven, my first reaction would have been anger, but God's first reaction was pain. A heart that loves is a heart that hurts, and God's heart hurt for the people following a course of destruction in their lives.

In the midst of this rebellion, God found one man whom He could count on. One man who would walk straight and keep coming.

> *Noah found favor in the eyes of the LORD. Noah was a righteous man, blameless among the people of his time, and he walked with God.* (verses 8-9)

Building It Right

You know the story of God's determination to start over and repopulate the earth with Noah's family. Preceding the great flood was an extended time period when Noah built the ark and preached to the people, warning them of the coming judgment.

Building a huge ship away from water must have made Noah seem like an eccentric fool to his neighbors. Imagine the cat-calls and cruel remarks! Yet step by step he moved forward, and some say the preaching and building process lasted 120 years.

Maybe today you are racing back and forth, trying to find satisfaction in staying busy, making more money, being with powerful people or keeping up an image beyond your means. Maybe you've selected a diversion that's destructive, and the consequences are closer than you think. God's heart hurts for you because He loves you. He wants you to enjoy the peace of faithfully following Him straight down the middle of the fairway.

Check Your Scorecard
READ PROVERBS 2:6-10

- What is the true source of faithfulness?
- What are the results of faithfulness? How have you seen these results in your life so far?

DIMPLES

EVERY GOLF BALL IS AT LEAST 1.68 INCHES IN DIAMETER AND WEIGHS no more than 1.62 ounces. From a distance, golf balls appear perfectly smooth, but they're actually covered with indentations called dimples. Golf balls are poor, defenseless, dimpled darlings at the mercy of big people with clubs who hit them with maximum force—sending them who-knows-where.

But why the dimples? The answer has to do with the flight of the ball. Without the dimples, the flight of the ball would be totally erratic. The dimples add just enough texture for the air pressure to keep the ball on a true flight path (that is, if you hit it properly).

Without pressure from different sides the trajectory would start to drift, resulting in constant inaccuracy and frustration. Not to mention more lost time looking for smooth golf balls in the tall grass.

Less Pressure, Please!
Pressure does have its benefits; it tends to keep us on the straight and narrow pathway. In the Bible, Daniel faced more pressure than most of us ever will. He wasn't overwhelmed by the tension; instead, he used his situation to keep himself flying straight.

Daniel was a teenager when the Babylonians devastated his homeland. He was taken into captivity with other young men to train for government service. This young man and some of his friends faced tough pressures that most of us will never encounter. He pursued creative solutions to problems involving substantial ethical challenges; and he remained willing to die for his core beliefs.

During his time of training, Daniel worked hard to maximize his abilities and prepare himself for greater service. At the end of his course, he received this evaluation:

At the end of the time set by the king to bring them in, the chief official presented them to Nebuchadnezzar. The king talked with them, and he found none equal to Daniel, Hananiah, Mishael and Azariah; so they entered the king's service. (Daniel 1:18-19)

Along with the training came the pressure to submit to questionable dietary requirements. The food set before Daniel and the other Hebrews was defiled because it had been offered to idols or contained ingredients prohibited by the young man's Scriptures. The external pressure to conform must have been great but the internal pressure to honor God was also great. These forces created turmoil in Daniel's life, which in turn helped him develop a creative plan. Daniel became proactive and offered this solution:

"Please test your servants for ten days: Give us nothing but vegetables to eat and water to drink. Then compare our

appearance with that of the young men who ate the royal food." . . . *At the end of the ten days they looked healthier and better nourished than any of the young men who ate the royal food.* (Daniel 1:12-15)

God honored their stand and strengthened them during the testing time. These men used the pressure of life's tension to fly past their rivals.

Thanks for the Pressure!

But what about the central issue of Daniel's life? What about his relationship with God? Daniel faced great pressure as he surveyed these options: Worship God and die a violent death in a den of lions, or deny God and live life with great authority and comfort.

Which would you have chosen? The pressure was powerful, but Daniel stood his ground. God's angel protected him, and he lived through the ordeal. The pressures of life that tried to blow him off course were counteracted by even stronger commitments to live worthy of the Lord.

Don't try to live a pressure-free life. It's impossible. Rather, counteract the world's pressure with God's strength and fly straight and long for Him.

Check Your Scorecard
READ COLOSSIANS 1:10-14

- What are some of the evidences of a life worthy of the Lord and pleasing to Him in every way?
- Which of these characteristics are a part of your life? Which ones would you like to become more evident?

DRIVING RANGE

IF ONLY GOLF DIDN'T TAKE SO LONG . . .

I've often thought that I'd like to take an hour in the afternoon and play 18 holes, but it just doesn't work that way. By the time I get to the course, warm up, play 18 holes, and head home, the better part of the day is long gone. I don't have time for carrying out the basic activities of life now, let alone trying to do it all with one less day in the schedule.

That's where the driving range comes in. I can leave the office, hit a bucket of balls and be back in my chair by the end of lunch—or pretty close to the end of lunch. I can work on my game, improve my form, enjoy the sunshine and fresh air. And be back to work within an hour.

Good Practicing?

Sometimes I enjoy the solitude of an hour without the phone, and sometimes I meet a friend and we hit and talk and talk and hit. By the time our bucket is empty, we've had a pretty good time and prepared ourselves for our next chance to play a full 18. Practice is crucial if we hope to improve our skill level, and that fact is echoed in the Bible. Consider 1 Timothy 4:7-8:

Train yourself to be godly. For physical training is of some value, but godliness has value for all things, holding promise for both the present life and the life to come.

Champions realize the need for training. The more we practice, the better we become—assuming we practice the right things.

Godliness, for instance, requires training; it takes practice and effort. Everything we need for godliness has been provided as a free gift, but we still have to haul our bodies out of bed in the morning to spend some time reading our Bibles and talking to God in prayer. The gift is free, but *making that free gift our own requires some training.*

Our natural self—the way we feel most comfortable—is in rebellion against God. We seek to protect and serve ourselves more than we seek to serve and honor God. It doesn't feel natural to do otherwise. Becoming comfortable with the idea of serving God and pleasing Him rather than ourselves takes time and training. As with any other endeavor, the more we work at it the better we get.

But *what* we practice is critically important! If we practice slicing the ball over and over, it starts to feel natural. Our slice then becomes part of our game until we unlearn and retrain ourselves in the proper swing. Second Peter 2:14 says,

With eyes full of adultery, they never stop sinning; they seduce the unstable; they are experts in greed.

The word *expert* is the same Greek word translated "train" in 1 Timothy 4:7-8. We can train ourselves for godliness, or we can train ourselves for evil.

It Starts with Good Thinking

The training begins in our minds. Practice starts as we discipline every thought to make sure we're becoming stronger in the areas that move us along toward godliness. This means we must discipline ourselves to avoid "the second look" at all the seductive materials that bombard our senses daily. The challenge of our lives is to become experts in thinking, doing and responding to life's problems and temptations with Christlikeness. WWJD— What Would Jesus Do?—must become more than a slogan. It should be a real filter through which all our thoughts and behaviors flow.

Hitting a bucket of balls in our spiritual lives means taking some time on a regular basis to get input from God's Word. It means talking to Him and expressing our love for Him through acts of service.

We don't practice in order to appease a divine wrath that we think lurks just beyond our sight. God is not a "worthy opponent" who looks for and exploits our weaknesses. He's on our side! He loves us and wants to go to the driving range with us—every chance we get.

Check Your Scorecard
READ PSALM 119:7-12

- How many things is the psalmist committing to do in these verses? Make a list!
- Which of these things could you apply to your daily life?

EIGHT

OUCH!

KEN, BEDFORD, SAM AND I ALL WORKED TOGETHER, AND WHEN THE opportunity arose we'd hold a special meeting on the course. Actually, we generated a few pretty good ideas on the green grass under blue spring skies.

But one day a par 3 took us totally out of our game. The hole was only 150 yards away, but half-way there a pond stretched across the entire fairway. No place to hide. The only way to play the hole was to hit over the water. Three of us got over, but Sam wasn't quite so fortunate. He hit a dribbler past the ladies tee that rolled within twenty yards of the pond.

A second chance—so he thought.

The rest of us walked to the other side, found our three balls surrounding the green and watched as Sam took his time establishing a perfect stance.

Then he went wild. Jumping, twisting, hopping around like a crazed bull. Eventually he pulled off his britches.

Little Things Can Sting
What would drive such an outstanding young man to such wild behavior? Why would he act so out of character?

Fire ants!

Sam had planted his feet in a fire ant mound, and instantly hundreds of the angry, vicious little critters swarmed on his legs. Sam's tranquil afternoon was demolished by the tiny invaders with their powerful, painful bite. These diminutive demons can make life miserable, biting hard and leaving burning welts. Yes, they're tiny, but their impact is painful and at times deadly.

Many little things can produce big pain and destruction in a human life. Take Judas as an example. Here was a man who walked and talked with Jesus for three years. He saw the miracles, heard the teachings and no doubt entered into many discussions that took place along the roads and over meals. Yet John 12:5-6 records a very interesting insight into Judas's life that demonstrates how *little* choices can lead to *big* consequences. A woman had anointed Jesus' head with oil. The perfume she used was very expensive—in fact, it cost a year's salary.

> *[Judas said], "Why wasn't this perfume sold and the money given to the poor? It is worth a year's wages." He did not say this because he cared about the poor but because he was a thief; as keeper of the money bag, he used to help himself to what was put into it.*

I don't think Judas started out with the goal of becoming the biggest villain in the history of the world. He just wanted to help himself to a little extra money. It was just a little thing at first; he was tempted and had an opportunity. At first he probably thought he'd just borrow the money and replace it when he could. But little by little the practice became a pattern, and the pattern became his lifestyle, and his lifestyle ended in suicide. He eventually betrayed the Person who loved him the most.

Don't Get Used to It!
The fire ant of embezzlement had bitten Judas, but he didn't react with pain. He just got used to it.

What little thing are you trying to get away with these days? What "no big deal" is getting ready to bite you and immerse you in intense pain? What little thing do you need to resolve before it becomes a destructive pattern in your life?

Judas easily rationalized his tiny peccadillo. He likely thought he could control his "small" sin and still keep walking and talking with Christ—no problem! Yet the impact was sudden, stinging, deadly. We look at the little ants and say, "They can't hurt me." Then we stand in the fire ant mound and wonder why we hurt so badly.

Take a look at your life for a moment. Take a look at the choices you're making. Examine the little things that seem so insignificant: the little lies, the little outbursts, the little insults will sting you. Get rid of them now. Don't let the little patterns grow into big, deadly character flaws.

Check Your Scorecard
READ PSALM 10:11-14

- Why do you think God doesn't judge sin more swiftly?
- Is there a little sin you should deal with before God intervenes? How will you confront it in the week ahead?

FORE!

OUR FOURSOME CONSISTED OF THREE PRETTY BAD GOLFERS AND one really good player. We were playing on a nice course in a housing development where my father-in-law had purchased a lot with the thought of building a retirement home some day. But for the time being, he played when he came to visit and provided me his access number so I could work on my game.

We were having a great time. Lots of lost balls, lots of laughs, a few good shots and . . . one memorable incident.

Why No Warning?

One of my friends (who had been hacking worm burners all day) decided that the foursome of old guys ahead of us was way out of his range; he'd go ahead and hit.

You guessed it. His shot was the best effort of the day. On one bounce his ball struck an unsuspecting player in the back of the leg. Ouch! He and his friends were hot! We got a major tongue-lashing (which we deserved) because none of us had the good sense to yell "Fore!"

Clearly, we'd been in the wrong. We had made a mistake and put the foursome ahead of us in danger. Fortunately, the only resulting injuries were the small bruise to the back of a leg and and a larger bruise to our battered egos.

Often the consequences in life are much more serious when warnings go unspoken or unheeded. Consider, for example, the story of warning hidden away in Numbers 22–24. Barak, king of Moab, summoned Balaam, a man to whom God revealed mysteries. Barak had heard of the Israelite's escape from Egypt and had seen them heading in his direction. He was terrified and wanted Balaam to curse them because he was no match for their military might.

Balaam saddled his donkey and headed for a visit to Barak. On the way an angel stood in the roadway, invisible to Balaam but visible to the poor donkey. The donkey stopped dead in his tracks, not once but three times. Balaam was furious with the donkey and beat the poor beast for not going forward. Then God opened the donkey's mouth—and the eyes of Balaam. The following discussion started with the donkey:

> *"What have I done to you to make you beat me these three times?"*
>
> *Balaam answered the donkey, "You have made a fool of me! If I had a sword in my hand, I would kill you right now."*
>
> *The donkey said to Balaam, "Am I not the donkey which you have always ridden, to this day? Have I been in the habit of doing this to you?"*
>
> *"No," he said.* (Numbers 22:28-30)

About that time Balaam's eyes were opened and he saw the sword-wielding angel in the road. The angel said,

I have come here to oppose you because your path is a reckless one before me. (verse 32)

What a Warning!

How often we start down a reckless, destructive path, and there is no one close enough to get in our way and keep us from going further! In this case, however, the donkey yelled "Fore!" but Balaam wasn't listening. He was rushing headlong toward disaster. The angel went on to say that he would have killed Balaam and spared the donkey. Yet Balaam was oblivious to the great peril he faced.

As Christians, we need each other. We need people in our lives who will yell "Fore!" when our pathway puts us at risk. Maybe we can't see the hazards lurking in our decisions. The power of temptation or our limited perspective blinds us to the full picture. Sometimes we are like Balaam and need our eyes opened. And sometimes we're like the donkey: We need to open our mouths and call out a word of warning to a friend who's headed for injury.

Check Your Scorecard
READ 2 TIMOTHY 4:1-5

- Does your buddy need a warning? How can you help?
- How would you describe the relationship between correct, rebuke, and encourage in verse 2? What does your friend need right now?

TEN

HAND-EYE COORDINATION

WHAT'S THE BIG DEAL? IT'S EASY, RIGHT? JUST STAND THERE AND powder the little dimpled darling a few hundred yards straight down the fairway.

No, it's not as easy as it looks.

All sports are challenging but not all sports are as frustrating as golf. When you play most other sports, you face an opponent trying just as hard to defeat you as you are trying to beat him. Other sports add the drama of head-to-head competition; an opponent can thwart you, make you mess up, even knock you down. But with golf there's no one to blame but yourself.

Which brings us back to that little ball on the tee.

Why is it so hard to connect a club with it and send it where you want it to go? It's called hand-eye coordination. You see the ball, you hit the ball. But seeing is not always hitting. A slice, a hook, a dribbler, even the occasional, virtually vertical "space shot"—in every case, it's purely your own fault.

Don't Seek Excuses

When trouble is brewing I'm the first to find someone else to blame. Surely my own incompetence and inability couldn't be the reason for this problem! Someone else didn't get the information to me on time. The other people in the group didn't understand the issue. Joe messed it up! Anyone but me is responsible.

However, like the game of golf, most of life gives us no one to blame but ourselves. This is never more true than in our relationship with the Creator of the universe. Romans 1:20 states,

For since the creation of the world God's invisible qualities—his eternal power and divine nature—have been clearly seen, being understood from what has been made, so that men are without excuse.

Woven into the fabric of God's creation is an ongoing story about Himself. Psalm 19 begins, "The heavens declare the glory of God." What we can't see about God, His invisible qualities, shine through in His handiwork in creation. We see the beauty of His design and the overwhelming power that resides within Him. We may never see the Master Craftsman, but we know a lot about Him by closely observing His craft. The sun, moon, and stars; the rivers, lakes, and oceans; the trees, crops, and grasses; the fish, birds and beasts—all of these tell a story. They each reveal something special about the God who made them.

We might say that God is more like a golf ball than a soccer ball. He isn't being kept from us as we chase after Him, desperately trying to get close only to have Him move farther away as we approach. He is waiting for us, propped up on the tee of creation, in plain view.

He's Seeking You

Of course the illustration breaks down because God isn't sitting idle while we look for Him. He is actively seeking us. He is proactive in His desire to establish a relationship with us and demonstrate His love and mercy in our lives. We are the ones sitting idle.

But we are without excuse. God's creation has given everyone on the planet enough information to be without excuse. The issue isn't *information*; it's *volition*. Will we determine to accept the information set before us?

Thankfully, God didn't limit our understanding of Himself to the general revelation in His creation. He also gave us His Word. The special revelation of the Bible gives us a crystal clear picture of God's sacrificial love for us and the response He desires. Creation leaves us without excuse, but the Word of God completes the picture for perfect hand-eye coordination. Yes, use your eyes to look for God in what He has made. But respond to Him based on the information at hand—already teed-up—in His Word.

Check Your Scorecard
READ ROMANS 1:18-20

- What invisible qualities of God can we understand by studying His creation?
- Who is without excuse? What does this mean for our world today?

ELEVEN

HOLE IN ONE

MY BROTHER PAUL HIT A HOLE IN ONE ON JULY 25, 1987, AT THE Laurelwood golf course in Eugene, Oregon. He did it on the 162-yard 9th hole.

I've never come close. I must confess that when he called me to share his good fortune, my response vacillated between joy and envy. I've hit a lot of golf balls and never had one go into the hole on the first try. This kid, two years younger than me, had stepped out ahead and left me in the dust. He was only thirty-two and I was thirty-four; these things are supposed to happen to *me* first.

But I still enjoyed his good fortune—to a point.

A Gateway Sin

Envy is a powerful emotion, and the Bible conveys several warnings about its destructive nature. Nowhere is envy's deadly effect more dramatically exposed than in the events surrounding the arrest and trials of Jesus. Pilate was a political leader who listened to the polling data and responded to the crowds. And because only the ruling Romans could authorize capital punishment, the religious leaders leveraged the crowds to support a death sentence for Jesus. Even when Pilate would have preferred to release Jesus, the crowd screamed for release of the criminal Barabbas instead.

Matthew 27:18 records Pilate's rather fascinating insight concerning these religious leaders:

For he knew it was out of envy that they had handed Jesus over to him.

The motivating force in Jesus' execution was the envy of the religious leaders who were bested in debate and whose traps Jesus had escaped. Their souls burned with envy, blinding them to the reality of God's Son and the opportunity to align themselves with His earthly activities. James 3:16 describes the impact of such envy:

For where you have envy and selfish ambition, there you will find disorder and every evil practice.

Envy is a gateway sin that opens us to other evil acts. As we compare ourselves to others, envy gains a grip on our thought patterns. As we focus on what others have and enjoy, we become blinded to the special gifts God has entrusted to us.

A Way to Stop It

How do we control the powerful urge to compare ourselves to others? How do we stop the rush of jealousy that destroys our relationships? Peter gives us a clue:

The word of the Lord stands forever. . . . Therefore, rid yourselves of all malice and all deceit, hypocrisy, envy, and slander of every kind. Like newborn babies, crave pure spiritual milk, so that by it you may grow up in your salvation. (1 Peter 1:25–2:2)

The command to rid ourselves of envy (and many other relational sins) comes sandwiched between two comments about the Word of God. The answer is easy to understand but difficult to apply. The simple answer is to read, study, and obey the Scriptures. The challenge is to grow up in our salvation by consuming the Word of God regularly.

The real loser is not the *object* of our envy, even though we can dish out a whole lot of hurt. Envy destroys its *owner*.

A heart at peace gives life to the body, but envy rots the bones. (Proverbs 14:30)

Envy eats away at our strength and stability. It destroys us from the inside, leaving us empty and hollow.

The next time your golf partner knocks down a 30-foot putt for birdie and you three-putt for double bogie, don't let the comparison eat you up. Let him enjoy the moment, and then move on to the next tee ready to do your best.

Check Your Scorecard
READ 1 CORINTHIANS 13:1-6

- Why do you think envy is the first negative characteristic used to contrast true love?
- When have you been able to rise above envious feelings? How could you apply that experience to a current temptation to envy?

TWELVE

HOOK SHOT

BEAUTIFUL HOMES LINED THE FAIRWAYS OF THE COUNTRY CLUB course where my friend had invited me to play. In spite of the lovely setting, though, I was a bit nervous. *Why do the greens look so small and the picture windows so huge?*

We navigated the front 9 pretty well, staying away from the backyards of most of the neighbors. But on the back 9 I hooked a drive through the yard and onto the patio of a home displaying three white signs with red letters shouting: OUT OF BOUNDS—NO TRESPASSING!

The tone was anything but inviting, but I could see my ball resting a few feet from the back door. *Maybe no one's home,* I thought. *I bet I can get over there and back before the owner notices.*

"Better not try it," said my host, as if reading my mind. "He's an angry old coot. Drop a ball and let's play on."

My game deteriorated over the next few holes, and again I hooked a shot into a beautifully manicured backyard. *Oh no,* I thought. *Here we go again.* Only this time the owner was at home. I could feel a lecture brewing as I approached the house.

To my delight, the retired gentleman tossed me the ball, chuckled, and told me, "More body—not so much hands. I get a lot of free golf balls from you guys who can't correct a hook."

Enjoying Grace?

What a dramatic contrast in attitude and style between two lot-owners on the same golf course! One man controlled his environment through fear, intimidation, and legalism. The other influenced his through warmth, openness, and freedom.

The contrast boiled down to one word: grace. In Matthew 18, Jesus tells a powerful story to illustrate our need to be receivers and transmitters of God's grace. A man owed his master millions of dollars. His investments had apparently gone bad, and he had no possible way of repaying his debt. The man begged his master to forgive the debt and not exercise his right to sell him and his family into slavery. With a generous heart, the master erased the debt even though it cost him dearly.

The reaction of the forgiven debtor is what shocks us. Instead of floating out on cloud nine and sharing his joy with everyone he meets, he becomes hardened and bitter. When he encounters a man owing him less than twenty dollars, he demands immediate payment, chokes him, and throws him into prison.

The witnesses can't believe their eyes. They report the incident to the generous master, who recalls his servant and reads him the riot act.

"You wicked servant," he said, "I canceled all that debt of yours because you begged me to. Shouldn't you have had mercy on your fellow servant just as I had on you?"
(verse 32)

The rest of the story is not a pretty picture. The greedy, ungrateful man suffers severe punishment for his actions.

47

Pass It On!

We've been forgiven so much. God's grace has washed away the debt of our sins so that we can stand before God clothed in His pure righteousness. We should be thrilled with our good fortune and ready to pass on our joy to others. Yet all too often we forget the joy of our salvation. Not only do we miss out on the chance to do back flips over Christ's goodness, we punish everyone around us and fail to offer forgiveness for the smallest offenses. Threatening punishment is easier than offering grace.

But which house do you want to live in? Do you want to hide in disgruntled gloom, expecting God to extend His grace to you but unwilling to pass it on to all the other hook-shot guys? Or do you want to enjoy the blessings of God's grace and share that joy with all you meet—even if they're out of bounds?

Check Your Scorecard

READ EPHESIANS 1:7-8

- What is the significance of the fact that God lavished His grace upon you?
- What emotions come to mind as you reflect upon God's grace for you?

THIRTEEN

WHERE'D IT GO?

GARDEN VALLEY IS A BEAUTIFUL GOLF COURSE LOCATED BETWEEN Tyler and Dallas on Interstate 20. Its bent grass greens, dogwood trees, and azalea-lined fairways look sensational, especially in springtime. Once, when my wife and I were helping host a charity tournament there, we had some free time after lunch to watch the golfers as they played the 18th hole toward the clubhouse.

One foursome provided the best entertainment of the afternoon. They hit their approach shots to within a hundred yards of the green, which was slightly up hill from their lie. They couldn't see the cup, but they had a fine view of the flag.

We watched as they demonstrated their short-game skills and sent their balls sailing toward the green. They had hit left, right, long, and right on target toward the flag.

The four men located the first three balls and then searched high and low, left and right, for the fourth golf ball. Where did it go?

Almost in desperation and frustration, one guy looked in the cup.

Great Expectations?

The next thing we saw was a series of high fives, accompanied by loud whoops and hollers. Of course, the intent of each of the golfers was to get the ball in the hole, but none of them expected it to really happen—at least not from that far out.

There's a parallel in Scripture. In Acts 12 we read an account in which the Christians were being persecuted by Herod and the religious leaders. The apostle James had been killed, to the delight of those who opposed Christianity. Next, Peter was arrested with the expectation of a similar fate. But that night an angel from the Lord entered the prison and woke Peter from his sleep. He escorted the apostle out of prison and turned him loose.

This was an amazing deliverance, but then things got even more bizarre. While Peter was in prison, the believers called a special prayer meeting. They congregated in a house in Jerusalem to pray for their friend, asking God to free him and spare his life. But while they were praying, Peter came knocking!

Rhoda, a servant girl, went to the door and heard Peter's voice. She couldn't believe her ears and became so excited that she ran to tell the others—leaving Peter standing outside. The reaction of the praying faithful is priceless:

> *"You're out of your mind," they told her. When she kept on insisting that it was so, they said, "It must be his angel." But Peter kept on knocking, and when they opened the door and saw him, they were astonished.* (Acts 12:15-16)

Where Are You Looking?

They asked God for help, but the last thing they expected was God's help! Do we have any room to criticize those early believers? We pray that God will resolve a problem or provide an opportunity, but we really don't think He will act. Too often we pray for things that are outside of God's will or for things that are less than the best He has planned for us. We don't understand all He is doing, so we think His answer "No" is "I don't care" or "I'm unable."

Or worse yet, we begin to think He doesn't hear us at all. We walk up to the green and look everywhere for the answer to our prayers—except in the cup. We ask God to teach us patience, but all He brings are problems. We want mature Christian strength, but all we face are struggles. We want inner peace, but all we have are troubles that force us to spend more time with Him. In our frustration, we may fail to see all of these things as "answers"—blessings that produce exactly what we've been asking for.

We must pray—God's will be done—and we must pray expectantly. Whether or not the ball lands in the hole is up to the Lord. But let's look expectantly for good things from Him. He has our best at heart.

Check Your Scorecard
READ 1 PETER 3:12

- Why do you think God is attentive to prayer of the righteous?
- What issue do you need to address before expecting God to respond positively to your requests?

FOURTEEN

LEAVING CLUBS

As a new golfer I was working on everything at once and getting lots of advice from my father-in-law. My drive was good on a par 5, leaving me in the middle of the fairway with nothing between me and more fairway. Then, on my second shot, my 5-wood felt great and the ball was still in play seventy yards from the green. I took my 9-iron, my sand wedge (just in case) and my putter with me, then I walked to my ball.

Head down, left arm straight, stance correct, grip just right, good back swing—and it worked again. I walked up to the green like I was supposed to be there. Leaving my 9-iron and sand wedge on the fringe, I looked over my chances at birdie (which were almost non-existent), watched the others putt, and then I had my chance.

Not even close to the cup but within range for a par. The sound of a par going in the cup is really sweet if you don't hear it often, and I was proud as could be.

Getting Excited
When we approached the next hole, my pride was quickly replaced with humility as I searched through my bag for my 9-iron and sand wedge. Not only did I look stupid in front of my father-in-law, but the guys playing behind us drove up in

their cart and handed me my lost clubs with a few embarrassing remarks and a good laugh at my expense.

The excitement of the moment can distract any of us. Joshua 6–7 tells of the man I consider the most forgetful of all times. Here's the setting: The Israelites have been wandering in the wilderness for forty years. The major activity was attending the funerals of all the people who had rebelled against God and chose not to enter the Promised Land at their first opportunity. The new generation had seen God miraculously stop the Jordan River, allowing the Israelites to cross unimpeded. God also flattened the walls of the first city, Jericho, and it had been utterly destroyed. But a special order had been given to the people. Joshua 6:17,19 states,

> *The city and all that is in it are to be devoted to the LORD . . . All the silver and gold and the articles of bronze and iron are sacred to the LORD and must go into his treasury.*

The spoil of this first victory belonged to the Lord. The next target was the small city of Ai that appeared to be an easy mark. A partial force attacked Ai and was soundly defeated. Joshua realized that God was displeased with the people, and he decided to investigate.

He Just Forgot

They discovered that a man named Achan had taken some gold, silver, and beautiful clothing from Jericho and hidden these under his tent. I can understand the great power of greed and the lure of temptation, but for his whole life Achan had seen the death penalty take its toll on the disobedient. A week before he had seen God stop the Jordan River so that he and a couple million others could walk through an empty river bed.

And Achan had had to scramble over the stones that God had just knocked down to get into Jericho. I can understand the excitement of the moment distracting Achan so that he forgot the events of the past. But seeing God work in such a dramatic way and then immediately forgetting—or ignoring—His direct command is amazing.

Sadly, I'm not so different from Achan. I forget the clubs that put me into position for a victory. The excitement and distractions of life cloud my memory of God's faithfulness and forgiveness, and I take for granted the protection I enjoy on a daily basis.

How is it with you? Are you letting life's dramas distract you? Don't become so accustomed to God's grace that you forget His directives for your life. Remember what God is doing in your life and respond with obedience.

Check Your Scorecard
READ PSALM 119:60-63

- What two patterns did the psalmist use to help him remember God's law?
- What can you do to remind yourself to obey His commands?

FIFTEEN

LESSONS

MY ROOMMATE HAD PLAYED GOLF SINCE CHILDHOOD AND MADE the team at a big-time university. He was willing to tutor me into the sport and pass along all the insights he had learned over the years. I was a challenging student, to be sure, but his efforts paid off—slightly.

Most evenings we hit a bucket of old balls from the front of our mobile home across a soccer field and into a horse pasture. He critiqued the position of my head, the location of my back swing, the grip for both hands, and the direction of my arm swing. There were so many things to think about; I felt awkward and self-conscious.

The one easy part, though, was knowing where to stand. I'd learned that lesson well, positioning my feet just right. You see, I could do that simple thing first, before having to worry about all the other actions that must follow.

Then it came time to play with my future father-in-law.

Torn Between Two Masters

I was a wreck. This was the man who had grilled me for two hours when I asked him if I could marry his daughter. He was a tough but good-natured businessman who always did things "the right way"—his way.

And he didn't like my stance.

"Your feet are too far apart," he said. "How do you think you'll ever hit the ball standing like that? Do it like this." And he would demonstrate the "proper" way to stand in relationship to the ball. The only thing I thought I had understood from my roommate's lessons was now shot to pieces. Now I couldn't even stand properly, let alone hit the ball!

Two teachers, two ideas, one novice unable to sort out the difference. In at least three places the Bible talks about the problem of one person being pulled in two different directions. First, Matthew 6:24 says,

No one can serve two masters. Either he will hate the one and love the other, or he will be devoted to the one and despise the other. You cannot serve both God and Money.

The call of money can be very strong, especially for men. We work for it, save it, invest it, and sometimes trust it more than anything else. It vies with God Himself for supremacy in our lives. Yet there can only be one master.

We're also reminded that two people who are linked together and yet have different spiritual commitments create a contest of wills. Second Corinthians 6:14 says,

Do not be yoked together with unbelievers. For what do righteousness and wickedness have in common?

Certain relationships can pull us away from God. Whether in marriage or business, a long-term commitment to a person whose life is not focused on loving and serving God is a recipe for disaster.

Finally, there's doubt, the kind that creates a double-minded situation. James 1:6-8 says,

But when he asks, he must believe and not doubt, because he who doubts is like a wave of the sea, blown and tossed by the wind. That man should not think he will receive anything from the Lord; he is a double-minded man, unstable in all he does.

The word *double-minded* literally means "two-souled." Doubt creates vacillation and tosses a person back and forth. When we come to God, we must pray with faith. We must not be pulled back and forth by our inner doubts and uncertainty. Yes, we all have doubts, but they must come to rest in the person of Jesus Christ. We may not understand the implications of the events of our lives, but we can take the next step with stable confidence in God.

Money, relationships, and inner questioning can keep us tied up in knots. They can paralyze us and keep us from moving forward with confidence. So why not take this stance: Today I will listen to the one true Coach and follow His instructions.

Check Your Scorecard
READ PSALM 27:4

- What does this psalm state as the focus of David's life?
- What is the one thing you would ask for if given the opportunity? Why?

SIXTEEN

LIGHTNING

TAKE LIGHTNING SERIOUSLY!

It's the first lesson golfers learn. Nevertheless, there are too many tragic stories of golfers caught in storms who seek cover too late—and are killed or seriously injured by a powerful bolt slicing through them to the ground.

Even a professional golfer was hit by lightning. Asked what he would do if ever again caught in a lightning storm, he is reported to have said, "I'd hold a 2-iron over my head. Even lightning can't hit a 2-iron."

Because of the heavy rain that usually accompanies lightning, the most natural tendency is to head for cover under a big tree. Relief from the rain may be helpful, but a tree can attract lightning—a much more serious danger.

Where's the Relief?

We all seek relief. We all try to find something that will make the rain stop falling on our lives. But often the protection we choose attracts even greater danger. Jeremiah 9:23 gives us a look at three places of temporary relief that may put us in greater jeopardy than we anticipate:

This is what the LORD says: "Let not the wise man boast of his wisdom or the strong man boast of his strength or the rich man boast of his riches."

Wisdom, strength, and riches are all places men turn to for cover; each hiding place presents potential danger. First, it is better to be wise than foolish. I would rather have understanding than ignorance. But wisdom and knowledge are insufficient by themselves. One more motivating seminar, another inspiring lecture, a few more books or academic degrees won't meet the deepest needs of our lives.

Second, many men see strength as the answer to life's challenges. This could include physical strength, but a bigger issue is at stake. How much power do we hold? Who reports to us? How many keys are on my ring? What information do I have that is inaccessible to others?

The third temporary form of relief is riches. In our materialistic world, the worthiness of the goal of "financial independence" goes unchallenged. The impulse to have more and get ahead of others may dominate your thinking. But when is enough enough? Why must we compare our house, car, and watch to those of others? When did we allow ourselves to be defined by our income and possessions?

There is nothing wrong with wisdom, strength, or riches. They are gifts from God. Problems arise when we use them for protection against the storms of life. We can't fight our way or buy our way out of all our problems. Wisdom helps, strength helps, money helps; however, they are only resources that God graciously provides. If we become dependent upon them for our security and worth, they can become sources of serious danger.

Here's the Refuge
What is the safe solution? Where can we go to find protection from the storms and not put ourselves in greater danger? The next verse gives us the answer.

> *"Let him who boasts boast about this: that he understands and knows me, that I am the LORD, who exercises kindness, justice and righteousness on earth, for in these I delight," declares the LORD.* (Jeremiah 9:24)

Run for heavenly cover! Our relationship with God must be the place we go for protection. God values kindness, justice, and righteousness, and we can nurture these same traits in our lives. Closest to God's heart are the character issues and attitudes we're developing, not the tin stars we accumulate along the way. As we work to become more like Christ, we will find refuge in Him and not merely in the gifts He has given us.

Life is filled with lightning storms, considerable danger, and potential disaster. If we hide under the protection of wisdom, strength, or money, we'll make ourselves vulnerable to even greater hazards.

Check Your Scorecard
READ JOHN 17:15-17

- What dangers are staring you in the face these days?
- What is your ultimate source of security? How have you trusted that security lately?

SEVENTEEN

LONG DRIVE

TERRY FARUM WAS THE LONG-DRIVE CHAMPION ON THE PGA TOUR in 1990. Now retired from the tour, Terry uses his talents as a golfer and showman to delight golfers around the country. My friend Britt Brookshire and I were working on a charity golf tournament, and Britt arranged for Terry to participate. Between the morning and afternoon tournaments, he hit golf balls through 3/8-inch plywood, from tees eighteen inches off the ground, and from a tee stuck to a board on my back. He was a real professional and a great entertainer.

Besides setting up a show between the morning and afternoon tournaments, we worked on giving all the participants a chance to meet and interact with Terry. We stationed him on a long par 5 and announced that because we were playing a scramble he would also hit a drive. Participants could use their own drive, or they could use Terry's.

Foursome after foursome came to the par 5. The golfers would blast away with all their might. Some hit great shots, but many tried too hard and sent their balls so far into the rough they will never be found. After the best efforts of the amateurs, our pro stepped up and powdered the ball, straight and true, right down the middle of the fairway.

Play His Shot

This looked like an easy decision for sure: Take the pro's effort and use it. Why rely on your own ability when there's someone who is much stronger and more capable, someone who is eager and willing to give you some help?

Scripture often speaks of God's resources being available to us and our need to humbly accept His provision. One of these resources is God's *peace*. We live in a world starved for peace. Broken relationships, shattered dreams, overwhelming pressure—all make peace a taunting phantom. Yet in John 14:27 the Prince of Peace says,

> *"Peace I leave with you; my peace I give you. I do not give to you as the world gives. Do not let your hearts be troubled and do not be afraid."*

The offer has been made, and the provider of peace has all we need. Not only is peace available, but *rest* is ready for us to use as well. Matthew 11:28-29 says,

> *Come to me, all you who are weary and burdened, and I will give you rest. Take my yoke upon you and learn from me, for I am gentle and humble in heart, and you will find rest for your souls.*

Rest is a rare commodity in our world. Peace is the antidote for the *inner* turmoil and tension that arise from unresolved issues that are our constant companions. Rest is the remedy for the *external* pressure that unrelentingly bares down upon us. We work harder and harder to accomplish. We believe we can have it all, but in the process we come close to losing it all. We play brinkmanship with our time, money, and energy, pushing everything to the limits.

Jesus is the pro when it comes to peace and rest. He worked hard, got up early, had late night meetings, and always seemed to have time for a needy beggar or a genuine seeker. Yet with all He accomplished, and the heavy load He carried, His reservoir of peace and rest were always adequate.

Along with peace and rest, we have God's power, as we're told in 2 Corinthians 12:9:

> "My grace is sufficient for you, for my power is made perfect in weakness." Therefore I will boast all the more gladly about my weaknesses, so that Christ's power may rest on me.

We all stand in need of God's grace and power. Our best efforts are insufficient, but His power makes our weakness strong. We can rely on our own peace, rest, or strength if we want, but God has all we need, instantly available. I suggest you play *His* shot instead of your own!

Check Your Scorecard
READ PSALM 46:1-11

- What does it mean to you that God is your refuge and strength? In what situations is this truth most real to you?
- What things will you trust God with today?

MINIATURE GOLF

I WAS SIX UNDER PAR ON THE 14TH HOLE, AND I HAD SEVEN HOLES IN one to my credit. My wife was two under, and my daughter was even par. Unfortunately, we were playing miniature golf and not the real thing. The steamy hot, east Texas afternoon had given way to a steamy, moderately hot evening, and a round of miniature golf seemed like a good way to invest some time as a family.

The well-worn course had known better days. The lighting cast a multitude of shadows, and most of the holes offered little challenge. But it was my daughter's choice, and we were having a good time. As much as I tried to stay focused on family and fun, I kept comparing this fake little course to the tree-lined fairways and manicured greens of a nearby, 18-hole real thing. No matter how low the scores, this was a big step down.

Bigger Is Better?
We all tend to compare the little, relatively shabby items of daily life to our grand expectations for the future and fond remembrances of the past. This is what happened in the life of the prophet Zechariah and the political leader Zerubbabel.

The children of Israel had rebelled against God. To discipline them and draw them back to Himself, God allowed the Babylonians to defeat Israel and exile many of the people to

Babylon. Then God mercifully allowed His people to return to Israel after seventy years in captivity.

The return demanded that the capital city, Jerusalem, be rebuilt and the worship of the true God be re-instituted. Reestablishing the formal worship patterns required a temple, but the magnificent structure built by Solomon had suffered extensive damage.

The people began building a new temple, but the grandeur of the past and hopes for the future created unrealistic expectations for this new structure. In addition, a strong beginning had given way to outside opposition and internal apathy. The project had been underway for sixteen years only to stall after the laying of the foundation. Then the Lord spoke to Zechariah:

The hands of Zerubbabel have laid the foundation of this temple; his hands will also complete it. Then you will know that the LORD Almighty has sent me to you. Who despises the day of small things? (Zechariah 4:9-10)

Zerubbabel would complete the temple, even though it would not be as magnificent as Solomon's structure, nor would it measure up to the high hopes of others. Hence the question: "Who despises the day of small things?"

We want bigger and better. We strive to do more, gain more, and go more while overlooking the wonder and uniqueness of life's little, seemingly insignificant pieces. But we dare not despise the little things.

Small Is Okay
What gives the little things value? Why are we attracted toward

the big and strong people and events while undervaluing the little things of this world? The answer is found a few verses before. Zechariah 4:6 says,

This is the word of the LORD to Zerubbabel: "Not by might nor by power, but by my Spirit," says the LORD Almighty.

The big and powerful people of the world try to do things on their own. The grand and majestic tend to depend on their own resources to accomplish great tasks and achieve great goals. Most of us aren't big, powerful, grand, or majestic, though. When we recognize that we are more like the miniature golf course—significantly limited and a little ragged around the edges—then we're right where God wants us.

When we admit our need for help, God loves to provide the resources we need. The Spirit of God is eager to work in and through us to accomplish the big and the beautiful. Don't be discouraged by what you don't have; rather, offer to God whatever small thing He has entrusted to you. God will not despise any offering. The Spirit enjoys empowering these gifts for His service.

Check Your Scorecard
READ EPHESIANS 3:16-19

- What is the relationship between God's love and His power?
- What small thing do you have to offer Christ today?

OFF THE DOCK

HITTING GOLF BALLS OFF THE DOCK AT PINE COVE CHRISTIAN Camp with well known author and speaker Tim Kimmel was a highlight of many summers. We set tees in cracks in the wooden dock and aimed over the lake into the horse pasture on the other side. Tim powered his share into the pasture, and I raised the level of the lake. The guests all got a turn as families cheered or laughed, depending on the outcome of each swing.

There was no point to the driving; it was just a display, an entertaining show of strength and accuracy. Nothing to win, just a chance to strut our stuff to the watching guests assembled on the balcony and dock.

Solid Impact Required

Making an impact on the ball, sending it to its intended destination, was the challenge in "dock golf." We wanted *every* ball to make it to the destination, but only some succeeded. Being a dad is a lot like driving golf balls off the dock. We hope that the impact we make on our children will be solid, sending our kids into a successful life.

In Psalm 78, Asaph, a musician who wrote several psalms, explores the impact parents make on their children as they send them sailing into the next generation.

*What we have heard and known, what our fathers have
told us. We will not hide them from their children; we will
tell the next generation the praiseworthy deeds of the* LORD,
his power, and the wonders he has done. (Psalm 78:3-4)

Asaph's assignment to parents is that they pass on three
things to their children: God's praiseworthy deeds, God's power,
and God's wonders. And there are two sources for parents to
draw upon: their personal experience and what has been passed
down to them from the previous generation.

Fundamental to our ability to pass along a godly heritage
is our own walk with God. We can't give away what we don't
possess. Children can easily detect flaws in our character. We
all have inconsistencies and weaknesses, and our kids will find
them. But the deeper and more real our relationship with God,
the more our children will detect the sincerity of our faith.

We are also expected to learn from others so that we'll have
an additional resource of information to pass on to the next
generation. We must tell them what we've experienced, and
we must tell them what we've learned from those who have
gone before us.

Solid Content Relayed

The discussion should begin with the praiseworthy deeds of
the Lord. As we see God at work in our lives, we praise Him for
His strength, wisdom, peace, and courage, along with any other
gift He has provided. The Bible is full of God's praiseworthy
deeds. We can share with our children the stories of God's work
on our behalf and for the benefit of those who trust in Him.

God's power is another reality to relay to our children. Why not talk about God's work in your life, how He helps you overcome temptation or strengthens you to face hardships? If we fail to give God the credit, our children won't learn how to recognize God's help when He provides.

We can also pass on information regarding God's wonders. The creation itself seems like a great place to start. Stand under a star-filled sky and remind your children that God knows each star's name. A walk in the woods will uncover the intricacies of God's design and genius.

His wonders are evident everywhere. But the greatest wonder of all is that God allowed His son to die in our place to provide forgiveness of our sins and the opportunity for us to have an eternal relationship with Him. Who will share this with the next generation?

Don't fall short when it comes to powering your children beyond where you can go. Impact their lives! Send them straight and long with information about God's trustworthy deeds, His power, and His wonder.

Check Your Scorecard
READ PSALM 127:3-5

- According to this Scripture, what are the parallels between children and arrows?
- What can you do to prepare your children for the next step in their spiritual development?

OUT OF BOUNDS

IT'S AMAZING HOW MANY RULES IT TAKES TO PLAY THE "SIMPLE" GAME of golf. There are rules about how many clubs you can have and when you can move—and not move—your ball. The rules also tell you about when and where to drop a ball, how to sign your scorecard, and who can give you advice.

I had played golf for about a year when I was introduced to the rule concerning out of bounds. I had been out of bounds a lot during my first year as a golfer, but I didn't understand the implication for my scorecard. Now I was playing with a real golfer who took great pains to explain why I picked up two strokes when I hit my drive over a fence and onto the highway running through the course.

His reasoning made sense, but I didn't like it. When a ball is hit out of bounds, it took one shot to get there and then a second shot would be required to return to the tee box. That makes the follow-up drive the third shot at the hole.

How frustrating! A two-shot penalty—and I'm no closer to the goal than before my errant drive.

Go Back to "Go"
When a shot goes out of bounds, the key to moving forward is going back. Back to where you started. Back at the start is the

security and safety of a clean do-over. The penalty strokes may be tough to swallow, but there is no way to move forward until we return and recapture the advantage of the starting point.

When we find that our behavior has gone out of bounds, there is value in returning to the starting point of the Christian life, as well. In Revelation 2, John brings a series of seven messages to churches located in what is modern-day Turkey. The first message begins with a basketful of compliments.

> *"I know your deeds, your hard work and your perseverance. I know that you cannot tolerate wicked men, that you have tested those who claim to be apostles but are not, and have found them false. You have persevered and have endured hardship for my name, and have not grown weary."*
> (Revelation 2:2-3)

This is an impressive list. This church is way below par and seems to be on a roll. These people are hard working, with a stick-to-itiveness that keeps them going. They are vigilant against evil, and they examine the doctrine they encounter to see if it is from God or from a false teacher. Does this sound like a church you'd like to join? It does to me. But let's look closer.

> *"Yet I hold this against you: You have forsaken your first love. Remember the height from which you have fallen! Repent and do the things you did at first."* (verses 4-5)

In all its busyness in Christian service, the church at Ephesus had forgotten its love for Jesus. The members had been so deeply involved in hard work, perseverance, fighting evil,

71

studying, and enduring hardship that they had lost their deep love for their first love.

Return to Sender

Maybe you have a problem similar to the one plaguing the Ephesians. Perhaps you've been busy doing lots of great things for God, but you've neglected your personal walk with Him. Take the penalty stroke and get back to the passionate love that characterized your original commitment to Christ.

The command is to repent. Repenting is basically turning around. The Ephesians were to go back to where they started— a love relationship with their Savior. They were out of bounds and had only one reasonable choice: Go back to the tee-box and start over.

So I ask you again: Have you felt a little out of bounds lately? Maybe you've been busy doing good things for God, but your love for Him has been cold and shallow. He sent you into the world to serve, but your acts of service have been purely duty-driven. He sent you to proclaim love and grace, but your words have lost the ring of sincerity.

The remedy is simple and sure. Realize where you are; remember your first love; return to Him.

Check Your Scorecard
READ JOHN 15:19

- What is God's attitude toward sinners?
- Is there any area of your life that requires repentance and a fresh start? What is the first step to take?

TWENTY-ONE

QUIET!

CONCENTRATION IS CRITICAL TO GOOD GOLFING, AND QUIET IS critical to good concentration. Golf etiquette requires that when a player is preparing to strike the ball, everyone else remains still and quiet. No sound, no movement, no distractions allowed.

Basketball thrives in a noisy arena. Baseball's roar builds with every pitch in the late innings of a close game. Football's cheerleaders pull the most sound possible from the fans. But golf wants quiet, making it quite different from most of the other sports.

A Time for Calm

We need quiet in our daily lives as well. Wouldn't it be nice to have someone raise a sign and squelch all the noisy distractions and diversions for a while?

Consider Elijah. The ancient prophet was coming off the biggest victory of his life. He'd prayed down fire from heaven and then prayed down rain to break a three-year drought. Instead of returning home to a hero's welcome, though, he was sentenced to death by evil Queen Jezebel. She opposed the true God Elijah served and was fuming over Elijah's victory. So Elijah ran into the wilderness and hid in a cave on the side of Mount Horeb.

In the midst of his fear and despair, Elijah received a visitor. God came and addressed the weary prophet:

"Go out and stand on the mountain in the presence of the LORD, for the LORD is about to pass by." (1 Kings 19:11)

What exciting events came to pass! First, a powerful wind ripped into the side of the mountain, tearing rocks from their places, tumbling them down the mountainside. Next came an earthquake. Soon a blazing firestorm roared up the side of the mountain.

The wind, the earthquake, and the fire were violent demonstrations of power—but God Himself did not reside in these displays. In each of these events, Elijah expected God to speak and send him a powerful message; the stage was set for God to pass by with glory and majesty. But after each of the three encounters, the same phrase recurs: "The LORD was not in the wind. . . . the LORD was not in the earthquake. . . . the LORD was not in the fire" (see verses 11-12).

The final event was a "gentle whisper." A quiet voice spoke to Elijah in calm, subdued tones. Elijah's life had been a series of windstorms, earthquakes, and forest fires. Showdowns with kings and false prophets created the adrenaline rush of his days during the recent past. He had seen God answer prayers and destroy enemies. Life had been a swirl of activity and excitement.

Now it was time for quiet. Time to listen for the Lord.

At War with Quiet?

God had supplied the power and energy for the events of

Elijah's life, but these events were not to be confused with God Himself. We may lead Bible studies, teach Sunday school, sing in the choir, or serve on the missions committee. These are all-important activities that have value as service toward God. But they are no substitute for the quiet time of prayer, meditation, and reflection with God.

Our world is at war with quiet. Television, radio, telephones, pagers, sirens, and the din of the city—along with our frenetic schedules and overloaded calendars—make times of quiet tough to come by. Because of all the noise, we need to work at setting aside time to refocus our hearts and cultivate the gentle whisper of God.

Don't fool yourself into thinking that the wind, earthquakes, and fires in your life are God Himself. They are merely helpers. By the workings of His grace, those things can draw you closer to the Lord. For your relationship with Him—the ongoing deepening of your fellowship—is God's highest priority.

So hold up the QUIET sign from time to time, and start developing a relationship with God built upon the gentle whisper. It's a sound too easily stifled amidst the cacophony of a busy, noisy life.

Check Your Scorecard
READ MARK 6:31

- Do you have a regular time set aside in your schedule to spend a quiet moment with God?
- What activities could you cut from your daily routine to provide a little relief from your busyness?

TWENTY-TWO

RECOVERY SHOT

TYLER, TEXAS, HOSTS A BIG GOLF TOURNAMENT EACH SPRING TO RAISE funds for the local university. The tournament is scheduled in conjunction with Dallas's Byron Nelson Tournament so some big-name professional golfers can participate.

When my schedule permits, I enjoy walking the course and watching the really good golfers. They appear to do what everyone else does—only better. They drive farther, pitch more accurately, and then drain their putts. But what amazes me the most is how well they get out of trouble.

My wife, Cay, and I were following Payne Stewart for a few holes, enjoying the power and grace of his well-trained ability. The par 4 featured a dogleg to the right, and the green was tucked back and to the left of the fairway. Stewart powered his drive and overshot the fairway, ending up in dense woods with the fairway on his right and lots of brush between him and the green. No way to cut off the corner and drive straight for the green—too much brush and too many limbs. Lay up in the fairway and then shoot straight for the green was the only option I could see.

But what do I know? Payne selected his club, addressed the ball, and fired a shot toward the fairway—with a massive hook that looped the ball within a few feet of the green. Up-and-down golf saved him par.

When You're in the Rough

He'd been stuck in a mess, with no good options, and there appeared to be no way out. Yet Payne got back on track as quickly as possible.

We all get into the rough in our spiritual lives. Rebellious acts of sin send us spinning out of control into dark woods and high grass. The issue is not whether or not we'll wind up in the rough; the important question is what do we do when we find ourselves there?

Israel's King David was no stranger to life's rough places. He'd been an adulterer and a murder, but his Psalm 25 indicates three essential remembrances for returning from the rough to the fairway:

> *Remember, O LORD, your great mercy and love, for they are from of old. Remember not the sins of my youth and my rebellious ways; according to your love remember me. . . .* (Psalm 25:6-7)

The first is God's remembrance of His own character. Certainly God is not forgetful, but David is building a case for God to respond to sin in a way that is consistent with His mercy and love. These character traits are central to God's revelation of Himself. His mercy and love motivate His gracious and forgiving response. If God were to respond by demonstrating His power and wrath, David—and all of us—wouldn't stand a chance.

Second, David pleads with God to *not* remember His

servant's sinful behavior. David's youthful sins would include the stupid, immature acts that would haunt him throughout life. But David also mentions his rebellious ways. These are the blatant acts of a rebellious heart. Sins of this type would include David's adultery and murder—horrendous crimes, premeditated and calculated. David begs God to remove these from the divine memory bank.

Finally, David asks God to remember him according to His love. In effect, David pleads: "Alter Your view of me, God, by filtering Your perspective through Your great love." Unless God sees him apart from his sin, David will be worthy of judgment. Thus he hopes that God's perspective of him will be based on love. This is his only hope of forgiveness, for David is totally at the mercy of God's love.

In light of David's experience, we can see that coming out of the rough has everything to do with God's compassion. But it depends on our willingness to initiate a request for forgiveness—with true repentance. Thankfully, our Savior doesn't respond grudgingly with a scowl and a "Don't let this ever happen again!" Instead, He throws His arms and nail-scarred hands around us and says, "Welcome home."

Check Your Scorecard
READ PSALM 103:11-14

- How does God's love relate to His forgiveness?
- What emotional response do you have to God's forgiveness?

TWENTY-THREE

RUNAWAY CART

THE SUN WAS SHINING, THOUGH THE AIR WAS COLD. NOT PERFECT weather for golf but good enough. The problem was I had promised to take care of our girls, ages six and two.

So much for golf.

On the other hand, where there's a will, there's a way. And I definitely wanted a way to play golf. I wanted to spend time with the girls, too, so maybe I could kill two birds with one stone. I bundled the kids in sweaters, mittens, scarves, and hats, and told them we were going for a nice ride on a funny little car.

The course was sparsely populated that Thursday morning, so we had little problem as I sat the girls on the seat next to me. Off we rode. They enjoyed the first few holes, but the excitement soon waned. We lost mittens out the back of the cart, and the girls were cold and crying. But hey! This was a father-daughter bonding experience.

By hole number 7 it had gotten ugly. I shanked my drive down the left side of the fairway and into a stand of trees. The tee box was located high above the fairway, and the cart path took a fairly steep angle down to a stream that cut across. I decided to park the cart on the path, and I walked forty yards across the fairway for my next shot.

I was almost to my ball when I heard the first scream.

79

"Daddy, Help!"

I turned to see the cart rolling down the gradual slope, heading for a steep drop to the creek at the base of the hill. My eldest daughter was slowing the descent of the cart as best she could, tugging on the side of the vehicle but being pulled along as it picked up speed. Meanwhile, my youngest was proving she had the strongest lungs in the county. Naturally I was on a dead run toward the cart. Fortunately, a worker nearby also heard the call for help and got to the cart before I did, saving the day.

That was the end of golf for the morning!

That was the end of me taking the girls to the golf course.

What can we learn from my adventure with the kids and the runaway cart? For me, the first lesson is to *recognize the danger of the downward slide*. Once the brake gave way, the cart headed for danger and possible serious injury. The movement was slow at first but gained speed with every turn of the tires. The downward progression of our spiritual lives will follow the same route. Proverbs 4:14-15 says,

> *Do not set foot on the path of the wicked or walk in the way of evil men. Avoid it, do not travel on it; turn from it and go on your way.*

The way of the wicked is a slippery slope. Once the pathway toward sin is selected, the pace quickens the farther you head down the hill. Get out of the cart and reverse direction as soon as possible!

Our Father Helps

The second lesson is to *realize the value of the cry for help*.

Reversing the downward slide is impossible without outside help. In other words, we can't produce real change in our lives unless our heavenly Father comes to the rescue.

When Peter's eyes focused on the winds and waves while he walked on the water toward Jesus, he began to sink. As he descended into the angry waters of the Sea of Galilee, Peter uttered one of history's shortest and most sincere prayers: "Lord, save me!" (Matthew 14:30).

Peter's only hope was to call upon God to reverse the (literal) downward course of his life. To avoid the danger of sinking below the waves, Peter needed to call for help. Jesus was ready, willing, and able to lift him up and restore him to a place of safety.

Safety is never farther away than our call for help. When we find ourselves on a spiritual downhill slide, when temptation is dragging us down and sin is pushing us toward serious danger—we can cry out for rescue. Our Father in heaven will be on the run to help us overcome the treacherous momentum.

Check Your Scorecard
READ PSALM 1:1-6

- What is the result of living on the slippery downhill slope?
- Is there anything in your life that requires a call for help? Suppose you uttered that call right now?

Scars or Smiles?

IT WENT SCREAMING STRAIGHT DOWN THE MIDDLE OF THE FAIRWAY, avoiding the trees on the right and the creek on the left. The only problem was that my ball was skimming the top of the grass. This was a real worm burner, rocketing along at top speed just brushing the tightly mowed turf.

I would play this shot, but it had none of the distance I deserved for such a powerful blast. After all, I'd powdered that ball! But when my brother-in-law and I approached, the problem became clear. I had cut a slice into my new golf ball that ran almost half way around it. Instead of striking it with the face of the club, I had whacked it with the edge, leaving an open wound and sending this ball to the practice bag.

Odd Combination

The scar was ugly, disfiguring, debilitating, and permanent. "Nice smile," said Roger, as he examined the damage. The curved scar resembled a smile of sorts, but what an odd combination: "scar" and "smile." When I think of scars—both physical and emotional—I think of something going wrong, usually very wrong. Sometimes scars are caused by an accident and sometimes by intended harm. But always they are a cause for tears, regrets, remorse, and pain.

Scars and smiles do go together, though. They have been

partners for at least two thousand years. Jesus' hands, feet, and side bear the scars of His love for us and provide the only hope of our eternal smile. Each of us carries scars, too. Certain wounds have left indelible marks on our lives as painful reminders of the effects of sin—ours and others.'

Hosea is a biblical book about turning scars to smiles. It begins with the story of a wayward wife pursued by a loving husband. The husband is none other than the prophet Hosea. The scars of his wife's sin affected her and their marriage, but Hosea's faithful love bought her back and restored their relationship.

The story tells a bigger picture of God's love for His people Israel, and it underscores an even bigger issue—the great truth that *God's love knows no bounds.* God loves us no matter how scarred we are, and He desires a loving relationship with us despite our past. That's why the final chapter of Hosea's little book can proclaim this message,

> *Return, O Israel, to the LORD your God. Your sins have been your downfall! . . . "I will heal their waywardness and love them freely, for my anger has turned away from them. I will be like the dew to Israel; he will blossom like a lily."* (Hosea 14:1,4-5)

The message was clear; Israel had a sinful history. The undeniable scars of the past could not be missed. But this is only the backdrop, not the story itself. The message is not that sin leaves scars; rather, it is that God turns scars into smiles. An offer of healing can only be for the sick and injured.

Good Transformation

The healing is based on one fundamental reality about our God: He chooses to freely love scarred people. His love isn't based on our beauty or ability but on His free will. He doesn't love us because we are good but because He is good. And His love is free, not based on our performance, our resources, our looks, or anything we think we can offer Him. He just decides to love us—scars and all. The scars don't go away; He just loves us.

Even though it's our sin that makes us prime candidates for His love, God has a wonderful way of transforming us. He loves to change us and grow us into effective servants for Him. God's love is like morning dew on the flowers of the field. This refreshing provision enables the lily to open up and reveal the full extent of its beauty. That's what God wants to do with each of our lives.

The scars are real and powerful but not as real and powerful as God's love for us. The results of sin are devastating, but the result of God's love is an ever-unfolding beauty that transforms our scars into smiles.

Check Your Scorecard
READ LAMENTATIONS 3:19-23

- What is your basis for hope in the midst of problems?
- Name a mark on your life that God can use for His glory.

CARRY THAT 9-IRON

LET'S JUST SAY I'M NOT FOND OF SNAKES. INDIANA JONES AND I have little in common, except for our dread of these slimy, crawly creatures. One of the first lessons in golf—just after "Repair your divot," "Don't place your shadow between the hole and the putter," and "Don't yell 'Hey, is that a bluebird?' during your partner's back swing"—is this: "Always carry a club with you into the rough."

Here in East Texas we have a full house of interesting snakes, a few that rattle but mainly ones whose patterns resemble dried leaves (copperheads) or ones that slither along the banks of water hazards (water-moccasins). So it's much better to reach into a clump of brush with the head of a 9-iron than your hand.

Be Ready!
Keeping a safe distance from possible danger is always the best policy. It's also helpful to have a 9-iron handy, ready for mortal combat with a belly crawler. Carrying a club along can help us do both of these things as we venture into the rough. Near the conclusion of Romans, Paul gives some personal advice to the readers about keeping away from those things that could injure or destroy. He says,

Everyone has heard of your obedience, so I am full of joy over you; but I want you to be wise about what is good, and innocent about what is evil. (Romans 16:19)

Paul is passing on some legitimate feedback to the Roman Christians. They are known for their obedience, and that has brought great joy to Paul. He says "keep it up" by doing two things. On the one hand, they need to be wise about the good things. We need to learn all we can about proper behavior, attitudes, responses, and patterns of life. We should go to the head of the class when it comes to doing good. We should work for straight As in obedience.

On the other hand, just as it was for the early Christians, when it comes to evil we should be as stupid as a rock. We don't need to know about the latest drug of choice in our society. We need not see the latest movie that would take our minds down violent and sensual pathways. There is much that we are better off not knowing because it's so difficult to unlearn the deeply imbedded impressions of the world. The bottom line: Keep a club's length from the sin that could bring pain and destruction to your life.

The club has another practical value as well: We may have to use it to kill an attacking critter. In the spiritual life, when evil inclinations present themselves, we are told to put them to death. Romans 8:13 says,

If you live according to the sinful nature, you will die; but if by the Spirit you put to death the misdeeds of the body, you will live.

A very simple truth, for sure, but also a great mystery. How do we kill an urge? How do we put to death those temptations that would love to sink their fangs into us and leave their debilitating poison coursing through our bodies? The answer is we can't do it on our own. We are weak and incapable of withstanding the attacks on our own. We need to allow the Spirit of God to have the authority in our lives.

Be Filled!

As believers, we are forever *indwelt* with the Spirit, but we are not always *filled* with the Spirit. Filling is totally an issue of our will. When temptations arise, it's great to have a club along to deliver a death-blow but that is a choice we have to make. If we choose to hang around and see how close we can get to sin, or if we try to engage in hand-to-hand combat, we're sure to lose. Only by God's power can we choose to live a life that defeats the temptations slithering toward us.

What does that look like, really? How do we activate the Spirit's protective power? First, we have to be prepared. Never go into the rough without your club. You can't pick and choose when the attack will come, so *always* be on the alert. Never assume that you are safe from temptation.

Second, when the temptation arises, mentally rely on God's power, not your own. Sitting alone in a motel room, calculating your income taxes or getting cut off in traffic—the attack can come at any time to lust, cheat, or explode. Just say, "God, I am weak, but You are strong. I can't resist, but You can. Help me do what You want me to do." In effect, it's the decision to loosen your grip a bit, just for a moment, while focusing on what the

Spirit is doing in you rather than on what the temptation is doing. It's the most basic exercise in living by faith.

Third, review a key passage of Scripture, such as 1 Corinthians 10:13:

> *No temptation has seized you except what is common to man. And God is faithful; he will not let you be tempted beyond what you can bear. But when you are tempted, he will also provide a way out so that you can stand up under it.*

Fourth, review the consequences. Ask yourself, "What will I lose?" and, "What pattern will I set?"

Finally, focus your attention on Christ until the temptation passes. Remember all He has done for you, and think about the obedient gratitude you can express to Him in a moment of prayer. If you'll follow these simple steps, you'll be taking your club you with into the rough. You'll keep a safe distance, and when confronted with urges to stray, you'll destroy the temptation by the power of God's Spirit.

Check Your Scorecard
READ MATTHEW 6:13

- Why must we pray to be lead away from temptation?
- What temptation is of greatest danger to you? How have you dealt with it in the past? What can you do differently in the future?

TWENTY-SIX

SQUIRREL

THE COURSE WAS CHALLENGING BUT NOT THAT DIFFICULT. THE FAIRways sported lots of beautiful hardwoods, numerous sand traps, and some water. But by far the most unique feature of the course was the squirrels. Their gray, bushy tails bounced across every fairway; they scampered over every green and chattered overhead from every branch of every tree.

Sometimes the curious creatures would romp onto the fairway to take a closer look at the golf balls as they rolled to a stop. Below the limbs of the pecan trees were the remains of many wonderful squirrel meals. The squirrels were everywhere, and that lead to the problem for my friend Eldon.

Eldon addressed the ball in the tee box as he had on the other holes, drew his driver back, and swung forward with his smooth, powerful swing. As happens from time to time, Eldon hit a screamer about six inches off the ground, and like a smart bomb it rocketed down the fairway until it collided with one of the squirrels (former squirrel, that is).

Two Destinations

The poor creature never had a chance. Eldon meant no harm to the furry little creature but, nevertheless, his time was up.

Death comes when we humans least expect it, too. What

happens when we die? Is the end the end? What awaits us on the end of life's journey? Most importantly, how can we prepare for that inevitable moment? Hebrews 9:27 says,

Man is destined to die once, and after that to face judgment.

This verse is filled with several important truths. Clearly, death is a certainty. Reincarnation is not an option; we only die once, but our existence continues beyond our last breath in this world. We will be held accountable for the decisions, actions, attitudes, and thoughts of this life.

There are more questions than answers when it comes to the details of the next life, but we know that there are only two options, two ultimate destinations—heaven or hell.

Jesus speaks about both. In John 14:1-3, Jesus explains to His disciples that things are about to change and that He will soon be leaving them. He says,

"Do not let your hearts be troubled. Trust in God; trust also in me. In my Father's house are many rooms; if it were not so, I would have told you. I am going there to prepare a place for you. And if I go and prepare a place for you, I will come back and take you to be with me that you also may be where I am."

Three important truths weave themselves through this statement. First, *the future should not be troubling and frightful.* The uncertainties that accompany the unknown must give way to the assurance that Jesus has the whole process under control.

Second, *Jesus is preparing many rooms.* The imagery requires some historical and cultural background. In Bible times, the prospective Jewish husband would use the time between the arrangement of the marriage and the wedding to prepare an apartment within his parent's house. The couple would live with the husband's parents in the family estate. Jesus is using this common practice to explain the care He's willing to provide to all who put their trust in Him.

Third, *the focus of heaven is being with God.* The uninterrupted union with God and the unassailable privilege of worshipping Him will make heaven heavenly. Floating on a cloud while playing a harp sounds like something I could get excited about for about fifteen minutes — but for all of eternity? This cartoonish imagery is far from what I expect God has in store for us. Whatever heaven is, it will involve thrills that surpass our wildest dreams. Central to this will be our unfiltered connection with God Himself.

One Way to Heaven
Thomas asks the question all the disciples were likely thinking, "Lord, we don't know where you are going, so how can we know the way?"

Jesus answered, "I am the way and the truth and the life. No one comes to the Father except through me" (John 14:5-6). There is only one way to reach the great existence God wants us to enjoy with Him. We must establish a relationship with Jesus in this life in order to extend it to the next.

The other option isn't as pretty, but the way is just as sure. Any pathway not built upon a relationship with Jesus leads toward hell — painful, eternal separation from God. Disaster awaits the most genuine person who sincerely follows any other route except the one provided by Jesus through His death on the cross.

The squirrel was minding his own business, enjoying a sunny day. Yet without warning, he instantly became an ex-squirrel. We'll all make an exit from this life (hopefully, without the word *Titleist©* or *Topflight©* tattooed into our foreheads). Therefore, we must not put off the issues that concern our eternal destiny until a better time. And, as Christians, let's look for opportunities to share the good news of heaven with those who need to settle the issues of their eternal destiny.

Check Your Scorecard
READ 2 CORINTHIANS 5:1-10

- How do these verses compare life on earth with life in heaven?
- What can you do to reach the goal of pleasing God (verse 9), at least for this day?

STILL YOUR TURN!

I COULD HIT THE BALL PRETTY WELL OFF THE TEE, AND ONCE ON THE green it was only a matter of time. But my short game needed work. One memorable hole found me just short of the green, and I was away. My next shot was well beyond the green, so I was still farther away than the others in my foursome. The next stroke sent me even more distant, and I started hearing the standard refrain from the guys, "It's *still* your turn."

Back and forth across the green I went—every shot making matters worse. One mistake led to another until I mercifully sank a putt to end the misery.

Hacking Away

I didn't intend to go from bad to worse; it just happened that way. Actually, I wanted each shot to be perfect, but the results were disastrous.

No doubt that's how it was with Judas, the betraying disciple. He didn't wake up one morning deciding to be the most notorious villain of all time. He just kept hacking at life, sending himself farther and farther in the wrong direction, until the wretched end.

Judas was the only one of the twelve disciples not from Galilee, so he probably felt a little like an outsider. Yet Judas was selected as the group's treasurer, the only office within the group. Did he want the recognition to make him feel needed and special?

Without pushing imagination too far, I think it's fair to say that Judas must have lacked strong friendships, had a significant need for acceptance, and sought to be special by being around Jesus. He held a position that probably made him feel good, and he was willing to work extra hard so that others would approve of him.

Sound like anyone you know?

I think Judas struggled with anger as well. In John 12:1-8 we read the account of Jesus being anointed with expensive perfume by an exceedingly grateful woman.

> *But one of his disciples, Judas Iscariot, who was later to betray him, objected, "Why wasn't this perfume sold and the money given to the poor? It was wort a years wages." He did not say this because he cared about the poor but because he was a thief; as keeper of the money bag, he used to help himself to what was put into it. (John 12:4-6)*

Mark gives a summary of Jesus' response.

> *"Leave her alone," said Jesus. "Why are you bothering her? She has done a beautiful thing to me." (Mark 14:6)*

In the accounts of this event in Matthew and Mark, Judas goes directly to the religious leaders to arrange his betrayal of Jesus. His response to Jesus' mild rebuke seems to be: "I'll get you for that."

Spiraling Downward

Most troubling to me is that I see nothing to indicate the others even suspected Judas. When Jesus announced at the Last Supper, "I tell you the truth, one of you will betray me," the disciples were saddened, and one by one they said to him, "Surely not I?" But I would have expected the other disciples to turn and point at Judas, saying, "I knew there was something wrong with you!"

The progression went from lack of friends and accountability, to striving for recognition, to simple pilfering, to anger, to betrayal. Stroke after stroke, Judas moved himself farther and farther away from his intended destination. At any point he could have reversed direction by asking for forgiveness. He would have been received with love and support. But the isolation left him vulnerable. And like a golfer who's overshooting a hill-top green, sending his ball back down the other side, Judas was incapable of pulling out of his deadly plunge.

And all the way down, he looked as good as everyone else.

Check yourself to see where you are in these important areas. All the while, look for opportunities to help a brother who, though he's swinging hard and often, may be hacking his life in the wrong direction.

Check Your Scorecard
READ PROVERBS 29:6

- What sins seem to be setting a snare for you?
- What can you do to move away from this situation?

THE SWIMMING 9-IRON

MY FRIEND (WHO WILL REMAIN NAMELESS) LONGED FOR A FREE AFTER-
noon to play golf. The pressures of work, family, travel, and even
church were mounting. He was long overdue for eighteen holes
of relaxation. His schedule cleared, a tee time became available
and his playing partner was free.

So he headed for the course. Finally! A chance to unwind
from the daily grind and enjoy the fresh air, green grass, sunshine, and friendship.

Great Expectations

The expectations proved more delightful than the experience
as his shots found rough, trees, sand, and water. Each shot led
to a growing frustration that ended with his 9-iron joining his
golf ball looking up at him from the bottom of a wickedly
placed water hole.

Anger, frustration, and stress crowded into an already too
tense life, and the cure became a crisis. What was intended to
bring relaxation triggered rage and resentment. My friend experienced a counterproductive result from his high hopes and
expectations. Not only did the afternoon turn out badly, the final
rash act of exasperation cost him dearly.

What can we learn from this sad story of the sunken 9-iron? Consider two possible lessons about life in general. First, we can remember that real pleasure never resides merely in the circumstances of life—especially not in short-lived enjoyments of sin. Israel's King David experienced this lesson when his plans for pleasure turned overwhelmingly destructive. The vast empire David built had consumed years of hard work and featured great military strength and economic prosperity. Perhaps he felt he deserved a break from the intensity of his responsibilities. He had taken care of everyone else for years and now, surely, it was his turn to play.

When he should have been leading his army, he stayed at home.

One evening David got up from his bed and walked around on the roof of the palace. From the roof he saw a woman bathing. The woman was very beautiful.
(2 Samuel 11:2)

For King David, temptation came in the form of Bathsheba. As you know, the moment of pleasure gave way to a series of sins that reached the depth of murder. The joy of the moment turned ugly as what was intended to bring pleasure opened the door to immeasurable pain. David crashed and went far beyond the kind of frustration that launches a 9-iron sailing into a pond. Rather, here was the great leader himself sailing into a quagmire of depression and despair.

Multiplied Pain

The second lesson is that a response of rage always multiplies the pain. Moses found this truth to be indisputable. He was a Hebrew raised within the ruling family of Egypt. While watching his countrymen being abused during their work, he responded with anger and violence, killing an Egyptian taskmaster. Instead of becoming the savior of his brothers, he became their enemy. Those he tried to help reported the incident, and Moses was forced to run for his life. The result was forty years of exile as a shepherd in the wilderness. One rash act, one moment of uncontrolled rage, one sinful act cost Moses dearly.

How much better Moses' life would have been if he had trusted God to help him control this one area of his life.

David looked for pleasure and found pain. Moses acted in anger and received severe punishment. When moments of frustration well-up inside, don't respond with rage. Count the cost, count to 10, and count on the Lord to provide the control you need to overcome the destructive urges of your life. (Then go back and get that 9-iron.)

Check Your Scorecard
READ COLOSSIANS 3:8

- What are the consequences of allowing anger and rage to go unchecked?
- Are you trusting a counterproductive method of dealing with stress? If so, what would be more productive?

SHOOT FOR THE FLAG

THE GREEN SLOPED STEEPLY UPHILL, SURROUNDED BY MOUNDS OF rolling green berms. The trunks of the trees behind the green were obscured by the elevated putting surface, but the branches arched upward providing a band-shell backdrop.

My pitching wedge was in my hand, but where was the hole? The only hint was the top of the flag fluttering in the summer breeze. The hole — my ultimate goal — was out of view, but the flag gave me a direction to shoot toward. The flag assured me that what I couldn't see was really there.

Invisibly Real

With the goal being out of view, I'd been forced to rely on the flag, which I could see. It gave me the confidence that by heading toward it I'd eventually reach my goal. The writer of Hebrews didn't play golf, but he understood the principle of the visible thing assuring us of what remains hidden (see Hebrews 11:10). Actually, the Bible tells us of at least three things that are unseen but very real.

First is God the Father. John 1:18 says,

No one has ever seen God, but God the One and Only, who is at the Father's side, has made him known.

Jesus came to earth for several purposes, but one of the key reasons was to demonstrate the reality and character of the Father. The mystery of the Trinity is way beyond any of us to fully comprehend, but we can understand that Jesus was the visible image of the invisible Father. In the upper room, just before the betrayal of Jesus, Philip made a request of Jesus:

Lord, show us the Father. . . .
Jesus answered: "Anyone who has seen me has seen the Father." (John 14:8-9)

Although the Father was out of view, Jesus demonstrated His character so that we could know God's attributes. 1 Peter 1:8 takes this a step further.

Though you have not seen him, you love him; and even though you do not see him now, you believe in him and are filled with an inexpressible and glorious joy, for you are receiving the goal of your faith, the salvation of your souls.

The second item hidden from our sight is Jesus Himself. Only a few of the first Christians ever saw Jesus during His physical life on earth, but Peter makes it clear that two things are available to all of us, even though we have not seen Jesus personally. One of those things is *love.* Based on what we know of His character and love for us, we can respond with love toward Him. *Belief* is the other thing. Even though we don't see him now, we can be absolutely sure of His existence because of faith in the Word of God and the rational evidence that supports the resurrection.

The third hidden item has to do with our final destination.

The goal was not to see the flag but to get into the cup. Without the flag, and with the cup out of view, I would have been directionless.

Really Incredible!

To see Jesus we need to study the accounts of His life in Scripture. The more we look at Him the more we will understand the Father. The result is that we move closer and closer to the joyful goal of eternal life with Him.

After the resurrection, Thomas missed the meeting when Jesus showed Himself to the disciples. He doubted that Jesus had truly returned to life. But later Jesus appeared to Thomas, offering him the opportunity to touch the holes in His hands and side. Then Jesus said, "Because you have seen me, you have believed; blessed are those who have not seen and yet have believed" (John 20:29). Are you one of those folks?

Check Your Scorecard
READ 2 CORINTHIANS 4:18

- How does a man fix his eye on something unseen?
- On what good things could you be focusing your attention today?

PLAY IT SAFE?

MY FRIEND TIM SEEMED TO LOVE GOLF MORE THAN LIFE ITSELF. He played all the time, and the only thing he enjoyed more than playing golf at the local course was playing golf in a tournament.

The Saturday tournament was a hundred miles away in New Mexico, and at fourteen years old, Tim needed his parents to drive him. Ordinarily this wouldn't be a problem, but his parents were out of town, and he was stuck.

Well not exactly.

The police stopped him half way to the tournament driving a hundred miles an hour in his dad's car. And to make matters worse, he was smoking one of his dad's high quality cigars.

He didn't make it to the tournament, and he didn't play golf for a while either.

Called to Passionate Pursuit

Yes, Tim loved golf and went after any playing opportunity with (literally) reckless abandon. Foolish for sure, but passionate all the same. Do you ever wish you could throw caution to the wind and just go after something with no-holds-barred determination? My friend Tim acted recklessly because he was

(a) focused on golf and (b) foolish. Jesus calls us to act recklessly because we are (a) focused on Him and (b) wise. Passionately following Jesus at all cost applies to our possessions, time, and priorities.

In Luke 9:57-62 three men come to Jesus with the intent of becoming disciples. Each hears the call to passion and reckless abandon for the kingdom, and each is confronted with the things he must leave behind in order to move ahead with Jesus. The first man must face his love for possessions. As they were walking along the road, the man said to Jesus,

> *"I will follow you wherever you go."*
> *Jesus replied, "Foxes have holes and birds of the air have nests, but the Son of Man has no place to lay his head."* (Luke 9:57-58)

Jesus must have read his mind, for He is challenging the potential follower with the fact that possessions must not be a concern for the radical disciple. Anyone who wants to become a follower of Jesus must accept the seemingly absurd premise that walking with Him is more important than making money and more meaningful than accumulating the things money can buy.

The second man has a different concern: his time. Jesus said to him,

> *"Follow me." But the man replied, "Lord, first let me go and bury my father."*
> *Jesus said to him, "Let the dead bury their own dead, but you go and proclaim the kingdom of God."* (Luke 9:59-60)

Here Jesus Himself extends a personal invitation: "Join the ranks of my committed followers, and do it now." Apparently, though, the timing was wrong. It's highly unlikely that the man's father had just died and that funeral arrangements were pressing. More likely, the man needed to stay at home until his father passed away—in order to inherit the family fortune! In effect, he told Jesus to come back later. Can you imagine that? Have you ever done it yourself?

Still another man came to Jesus wanting to become a disciple. But his problem was his priorities.

> *"I will follow you, Lord; but first let me go back and say good-by to my family."*
>
> *Jesus replied, "No one who puts his hand to the plow and looks back is fit for service in the kingdom of God."*
> (Luke 9:61-62)

This request is similar to that of the second man's, but this time the emphasis is not timing but priorities. In the next verses Jesus appoints seventy-two of the most committed followers and sends them out, two by two. If this third man wants to enter the Lord's service, he must choose what takes priority and he must do it immediately. The opportunity for inclusion will not wait—he must choose now.

These three men had opportunities of a lifetime, but they had to make tough choices, too. They needed to set aside their needs for security and satisfaction if they were to follow Christ with passion, throwing caution to the wind. Would they risk everything to follow Him? The Bible doesn't tell us the rest of the story but it gives the impression that these three were not among the seventy-two disciples who followed Jesus no matter what the cost.

Do we want to be disciples bad enough to risk some money, time, or established priorities? Or do we seek the safe, secure path that in reality is a very dangerous choice?

My friend Tim took a big, foolish risk just to play a little more golf. We have much more at stake. We hear the call of Christ every day. And our tendency is to protect ourselves, following halfheartedly from a safe distance. Yet how safe is that really?

Check Your Scorecard
READ LUKE 5:27-28

- How was Levi different from the three men in Luke 9?
- What things might be keeping you from following Jesus totally? What does "totally" mean to you in practical terms?

THIRTY-ONE

SAFETY SHIELD

THE DRIVING RANGE LAY TO THE NORTH OF THE TENTH FAIRWAY, separated by a row of huge trees — poplars, elms, and oaks. The branches were intertwined and the thick matting of leaves made an impenetrable shield against errant golf balls escaping from the range.

On the other side of the range was a major highway. A massive screen loomed close by, supported by extra tall telephone poles erected to keep slicing golf balls off the windshields of oncoming cars. Keeping the ball away from unsuspecting golfers to the south and from innocent motorists to the north was a high priority of the course owners. Besides wanting to avoid the legal repercussions of an avoidable accident, they wanted guests to feel safe. They also hoped the course's image within the community would never be tarnished by an unfortunate injury.

In the Protection Business

Time and time again golfers would challenge the trees on the left and the fence on the right. Sending a shot into the trees or the screen was a common, though not intentional, occurrence. Time and again the trees and the screen protected those who needed it, though they may not have been aware of the danger.

God is in the business of protecting us as well. At least three types of protection are mentioned in the Bible. First is God's care in the face of physical harm. Psalm 121:5-7 says,

The LORD watches over you—the LORD is your shade at your right hand; the sun will not harm you by day, nor the moon by night. The LORD will keep you from all harm— he will watch over your life.

The problems of life will always be filtered through the protective shade of God's love. Psalm 121 is a psalm of ascent sung during the three annual pilgrimages to Jerusalem. Most of the population lived to the north of Jerusalem, so the hot afternoon sun would be on the right side of the travelers as they made their way to the big city. The imagery implies that God would be like a filter, providing sufficient protection so the deadly impact of the sun's rays would not create sunstroke on the journey or utter destruction in life.

Second, we see God's protection when it comes to the temptations we face. First Corinthians 10:13 says,

No temptation has seized you except what is common to man. And God is faithful; he will not let you be tempted beyond what you can bear. But when you are tempted, he will also provide a way out so that you can stand up under it.

The promise is not that we will avoid temptation but that we will be able to stand up to its testings. God will screen the temptations so that only those we can withstand will come our way. His protection is to help us bear up under the attack. To be a member of God's army is to expect to come under attack, but He will provide protection on all sides if we rely on His help.

Finally, we see God's ultimate protection in Psalm 91:1,4.

He who dwells in the shelter of the Most High will rest in the shadow of the Almighty. . . . He will cover you with his feathers, and under his wings you will find refuge; his faithfulness will be your shield and rampart.

This passage explains the basis of God's protection by using two beautiful word pictures. First, a pilgrim in those days was under the care and protection of his host while he visited his friend or relative. As long as the visitor was dwelling in the tents of his host, all of his needs were met. The safety and comfort of the traveler were the responsibility of the host. God says, "Dwell with me. I'll protect and care for you."

The second picture is that of a hen offering her body to protect her chicks from storms, fire, or predators. The mother would gladly lay down her life for her babies because of her great love.

Isn't that what happened? Didn't Jesus take our greatest danger, the punishment for our sins, and give His life to protect us? He screened the deadly impact of our sin's punishment with His own body. Now all we need to do is respond with a grateful heart and accept His gift.

God is in the business of protecting us from the things that would destroy us—physically yes, but more importantly, spiritually. If you have never done it, ask God today to provide His protection for you—eternally—by accepting Jesus as your Protector from sin's penalty.

Check Your Scorecard
READ PSALM 18:30

- What do God's perfect way and flawless law have to do with His protection?
- Is there a situation looming in your life that will require God's protection? What will it "look like" for you to trust Him in that situation?

About the Author

DAN BOLIN IS THE PRESIDENT OF DAN BOLIN RESOURCES, INC., which provides ministry, marketing, management, and fundraising support to Christian nonprofit ministries. He is also a senior associate with the Goehner Resource Group and a regional representative for Christian Camping International.

Dan earned his bachelor's degree from Seattle Pacific University and his master's of theology degree from Dallas Theological Seminary. He also holds an MBA from LeTourneu University.

A frequent speaker both nationally and internationally, Dan is the author or coauthor of several books, including *The Winning Run, The One That Got Away, Avoiding the Blitz, How to Be Your Daughter's Daddy, How to Be Your Little Man's Dad,* and *How to Be Your Wife's Best Friend.* He has also been published in *Decision Magazine* and *The Journal of Christian Camping.*

Dan, his wife Cay, and their daughter Haley live near Tyler, Texas, where he serves as an elder at Bethel Bible Church and as a board member of Dan Anderson Ministries and the Tyler Independent School District.

If you liked A HOLE IN ONE, you'll love these other books by Dan Bolin.

The Winning Run

Are you hitting home runs in the field but striking out with God? Dan Bolin combines real life experiences on the field with God's perspectives on life to create a devotional you can't put down!

The Winning Run
(Dan Bolin) $10

Avoiding the Blitz

Gain yardage on the field of life with this devotional. Discover how your love of football can help you apply a spiritual truth and lesson for life in under ten minutes each day!

Avoiding the Blitz
(Dan Bolin) $10

The One That Got Away

Designed for under ten minutes of daily reading, each section of this "catchy" devotional highlights an element of fishing. Apply a spiritual truth and lesson for your life through interesting stories about your favorite sport.

The One That Got Away
(Dan Bolin) $10